MOOG'S
MUSICAL EATERY

MOOG'S MUSICAL EATERY

BY SHIRLEIGH MOOG

A COOKBOOK FOR CAREFREE ENTERTAINING

THE CROSSING PRESS, TRUMANSBURG, N.Y.

Cover, Tom Parker
Book Design, Karl Wolff
Illustrations, Kate Lanxner

Library of Congress Cataloging in Publication Data

Moog, Shirleigh, 1936---
    Moog's musical eatery.

    (The Crossing Press series of cookbooks)
    Includes index.
    1. Cookery. 2. Menus. 3. Entertaining.
I.   Title.
TX715.M817   642'.41   78-5906
ISBN 0-89594-000-0
ISBN 0-89594-001-9 pbk.

Contents

When I married my husband, I decided almost immediately that he was too unusual a human being to be called just Robert or Bob. I asked him if he minded me calling him Moog, and Moog it has been ever since. If he had never invented the Synthesizer, I would still think he was a wonderful human being.

This book is dedicated to Moog, whose interests have made my life rutless, and to all the guests whose company I have enjoyed.

Thanks also to my Mom for encouraging me and giving me free use of the kitchen from the tender age of eight. She must receive the credit for instilling in me an appreciation of quality food. My parents never had a lot of money, but my mother always bought the freshest meats, vegetables and breads. I have added much to her cooking in the way of my own tastes, but my base is like hers--fresh, tasty foods.

I am also grateful to Peter Kubelka, a German film-maker and cook, who once told an audience that he considered cooking to have all the requirements of an art form since it had complexity and dynamics. Since I am a long frustrated artist, this made me feel just fine.

Thanks also to our four children for letting us enjoy our guests with a great degree of peace; my friend Cora for sending me a blank book which prompted me to stop procrastinating and start writing this manuscript; and my publishers for having faith in me.

Foreword

People sometimes feel they have to serve guests something more special and elaborate than family fare. They experiment with something new and, even if the dish turns out well, their anxiety is still apparent to everyone. It is really best to make something you are comfortable with and do well. You will be more relaxed and self assured, and so will your guests.

Fussing over people is really not a compliment. It's better to put guests at ease by being at ease yourself. My husband and myself are very informal people who don't enjoy dressing up or consciously trying to impress people. The dinners I've enjoyed most have been relaxed natural affairs where tasty fare has been served and people have been relaxed enough to enjoy each other

My husband, Robert Moog, started his Synthesizer factory in Trumansburg (a small town in upstate New York) in 1963. We had two children, very little money and a steady stream of musicians and artists to feed. My love of a challenge kept the kitchen smelling good, the palate happy and the pocket-book intact. My aim was to serve tasty meals that didn't strain me to the point that I was too tired or tense to enjoy our guests. If the food and camaraderie were good, a bit of disarray or dust was unimportant. I tried to have the dining room clean and attractive, but everything else depended on how much time was available. A catnap for the hostess will do more for the ambiance of entertaining than having all the beds made or the floor scrubbed.

Since 1963, I've fed hundreds of hungry musicians, painters, dancers, sculptors and film-makers. I've enjoyed it immensely and am grateful for the input gained from contact with them. The meal for me is never more important than the guests— guests are the *pièce de résistance.*

The most concrete affirmation I ever had as a hostess occurred when a film-maker friend of ours came early for dinner. He was very tired and slept soundly on the couch for an hour while I continued dinner preparations. It was one of the warmest compliments I've ever been paid.

This book is a collection of my tried and true recipes–dishes I have made often, without a long period of preparation. They are easy to make and have pleased a variety of people. I would like to share them with you, as good friends share their recipes. I hope this will become the book you will reach for automatically when you hear the words, 'Can I bring a friend home to dinner?'

May these recipes serve you as well as they have served me.

Shirleigh Moog

A word about quantities. These recipes may be halved or doubled as you wish, but I do offer a few words of caution. Some recipes (like Veal Dagmar) take a great deal of preparation time. I would not suggest you make them for more than eight to twelve people.

Please read recipes carefully. Make sure you aren't making much more work for yourself when you double recipes. It isn't always as simple as putting more ingredients in a pot.

Kitchen & Dining Notes

Kitchen & Dining Notes

Preferences

Fresh Foods

Generally I prefer to cook with fresh foods: herbs, spices, cheese, coffee, pepper, etc. The reason is simple. Fresh foods taste better. Sometimes I run out of a fresh ingredient and have to compromise, but I prefer not to.

Breads

Good bread is hard to find. Breads that are free of artificial ingredients are beginning to show up in supermarkets but they can't approach the texture of homemade bread. If you live near a bakery that makes tasty, wholesome bread, you're in luck, but be careful. Even bakeries use artificial colors and flavorings. Some even use cocoa to color pumpernickel.

It's worth finding good recipes for yeast breads and quick breads that can be made in quantity in a short space of time. I have included many of my favorites in this book. Children find bread making fun. Mine help me keep the freezer well stocked so that I never run out.

Butter

Butter tastes better than margarine. Since taste is what
cooking is all about, use butter.

Cheese

It's a mystery to me why anyone would want to buy
processed cheese. It looks and tastes just like plastic.
Moreover, it's almost the same price as natural cheese.

I refuse to buy any kind of cheese in a plastic pack. I
shop in stores specializing in dairy products which carry
cheese in bulk. They display large chunks of cheese and
will cut off as much as you want. Many natural food stores
and food co-ops do the same. Frequently, if I like a certain
cheese a lot, I'll buy the entire piece. Most stores will give
you a discount when you buy in bulk like this.

My favorites for eating at table with bread or crackers and
fruit are sharp cheddar, Swiss, colby, Danish Port Salut, bleu,
Limburger, brick, provolone, Liederkranz and Brie. As for
grated cheese, I always buy Italian varieties by the piece.
Almost any fairly firm cheese can be grated, but the Italian

cheese like Romano (sharp) or Parmesan (milder) are to my mind the best. A friend of mine who was born in Italy tells me his mother always passed the cheese with a grater at table. Now that is fresh! The taste is far superior to anything you can shake out of a container.

Fruits & Vegetables

These are best tasting when they are purchased fresh, especially when they are in season. Home canned fruits and vegetables come next in preference; then frozen fruits and vegetables, properly cooked.

Herbs

Some stores carry freshly dried herbs in bulk at harvest time. These are preferable by far to commercially dried herbs. I have been able to buy basil, sesame seeds, fennel seeds and bay leaves this way. The herbs are usually fresher, better tasting and less expensive

If you can get garden fresh herbs like parsley, basil, dill and oregano, you can use them fresh and dry whatever you have left over. The best way to do the drying is to hang the herbs in paper bags (to keep the dust off the leaves) in a warm, dry place. When the herbs are thoroughly dry, you can strip the leaves off the twigs and store them in small jars with tight fitting lids. Crumble the dry leaves before you use them in cooking.

I prefer fresh Italian parsley with its broad flat leaves to its curlier, *shyer tasting cousin*, common parsley. In wintertime when fresh parsley isn't available, I use dried celery leaves. I chop the celery leaves in fine pieces and store them on a paper towel over a metal grate. The leaves dry within two days and can be stored in a jar. They have a zestier taste than commercially dried parsley.

Marmite

This is a brand name for a blend of brewer's yeast flavored with salt, carrots, onions and spices. It's fine for giving body to soups, stews or gravies. It is especially good spread very thin on rye bread with a slice of cheese on top.

Meat Loaf Mix

Meat loaf mixture is called for in several recipes (Swedish and Italian Meatballs, Stuffed Tufoli, Meat Pie Yannina, and Stuffed Cabbage Leaves). It is a mixture of beef, pork and veal commonly available in your supermarket or butchershop. This mixture has a delicate taste which lets the subtle flavor of the herbs come through clearly.

Mustard

Grey Poupon Dijon is my favorite. I buy six jars at a time so that I never have to make do with the tasteless stuff that comes in other jars labeled 'mustard'. My children used to ask why I didn't buy the tasteless kind they serve in school cafeterias. I always turned their question around by saying, "That's exactly why - - it has no taste!"

Oils

Olive oil is the best, and the best olive oil I know of is
Filippo Berio. It's costly and getting more so, but from
my experience, second best isn't worth the few pennies
you save. Good olive oil has a greenish cast and a wonderful taste. When you step down to a cheaper olive oil, that
wonderful taste disappears.

Olive oil, due to its strong personality, is not desirable in
baking. I use corn oil instead. It's blander.

Soy Sauce

The soy sauce sold in supermarkets is an artificially colored,
foul-tasting blend, with a lot of salt added. I recommend
Kikkoman Soy Sauce, regular and light. I am partial to the
light variety which has a more subtle taste. You might inquire
about other good brands at the nearest oriental food shop.
The owners are usually happy to see someone genuinely
interested in far eastern foods and will be happy to help
you select what you want.

Waste Not, Want Not

Bread

Save stale bread, cake, cookies and dry cereal crumbs for making stuffing, croutons, bread crumbs and bread pudding (see page 184).Place them in a plastic bag, tie the bag securely and keep the bag in the freezer until you need it.

Broth

Broth from leftover soups, vegetable cooking fluid and stock from cooked poultry can be saved for later use to enrich soups stews, noodles, rice, etc. A convenient way to store broth is to freeze it in ice cube trays, remove the cubes and place them in a plastic bag, properly labeled as to the source of the stock. Place the bag in the freezer until you need broth.

Chicken Fat

When you buy a chicken and it happens to have some fat on it, cut the fat away from the meat and fry it over low heat. Add one or two tablespoons of chopped onion and fry til all the fat is melted. When the rendered fat is cool, pour it into a plastic container with a lid and freeze. This fat is delicious for frying onions, noodles, liver, veal, omelettes, etc.

Chicken Giblets

These should be saved and used for chopped chicken liver spread (see page 146). They can also be cooked with chicken fat and eaten on the spot or frozen in the raw state for later use in chicken broth or stock. (Cooked or raw, giblets are very good dog and cat food).

If giblets are cooked in a soup, all but the neck can be pulverized in a blender with some of the soup stock to make a fine gravy. (See page 65 for Giblet Gravy.)

Chicken Necks & Backs

Watch your butcher's display case for chicken necks and backs.
The backs are usually loaded with fat which you can render and
use later. Moreover, the backs and necks make a fine, inexpensive base for chicken soup - - they have enough meat on them
to make a good meaty soup at low cost.

Time

It's most important not to waste time. Since most of the work
in cooking lies in taking out the ingredients and arranging them
for use, you should make double batches of recipes that can be
frozen or stored. This practice is especially important for people
who like to entertain and don't always receive advance notice.
   There are many recipes scattered through this book for things
that can be stored for a long period of time in the freezer, refrigerator or on your kitchen shelf. At the head of each chapter,
I have asterisked recipes that can be frozen. Bread and muffins
(but not popovers) can be frozen with no loss of flavor or texture.
Jams or jellies can be either frozen or canned. Brandied fruit,
brandy balls, sherried cheese spread, nesselrode sauce, ratatouille,
are some of my favorites.

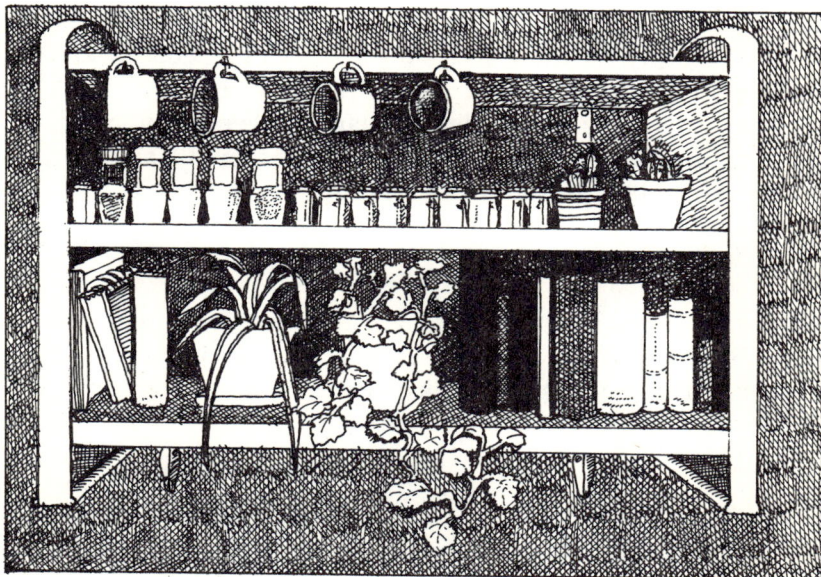

Functional Kitchens & Dining Rooms

Dishes & Glassware

It seems to me there are enough things in life to worry about without asking for more. I'm not the type to use expensive china and then worry about possible breakage. My glasses and plates have to be inexpensive so that if they get broken, it won't matter.

I do have some wonderful old crystal that belonged to Moog's Aunt Emma. It's thin and sings when tapped or rubbed. I love it for its beauty and for its link to the past. I always wash it by hand and have broken only one piece in ten years. I'd never buy it for myself, however.

On most occasions we use twelve ounce glasses with heavy bottoms. Ball-shaped, they are sometimes called roly-polys. They are inexpensive and extremely functional.

Water spots are a problem, but because I love seeing the color of wine through the glass, I haven't bought ceramic tumblers. Maybe I can learn not to mind the spots.

I own two sets of dishes. One is stark white and costs $44 for a service of twelve. The other is brownish stoneware that cost $75 for a service of twelve. We almost never entertain crowds so large that these dishes together can't handle it. If we ever do, I'd consider paper plates or rented china.

I have lusted after teak plates and hand made pottery, but I never did find a reason to go out and actually buy them. My brown and white sets do the job very well.

Tablecloths

White tablecloths set with crystal are not my style. I find Indian bedspreads and use them as tablecloths or I buy several yards of African prints and batiks. Some are large free prints, others are geometrics - - I love them all.

If I ever get tired of them, they can always be used for curtains, summer dresses or bedspreads. A setting of white dishes on a print cloth is about as formal as I ever get.

Placemats

There are so many pretty placemats available that it's easy to go overboard. Most of the time they aren't efficient because of the size of my family and the frequency with which I entertain. But when I do use placemats, I get the woven grass kind. They look natural and cool on a wooden table in the summertime.

Napkins

I use cloth napkins most of the time. They feel good and are in the long run cheaper than paper napkins. They are also less wasteful of natural resources. If possible, I buy them on sale to match or contrast with the tablecloths I own. I prefer prints - - grease spots get lost in the design.

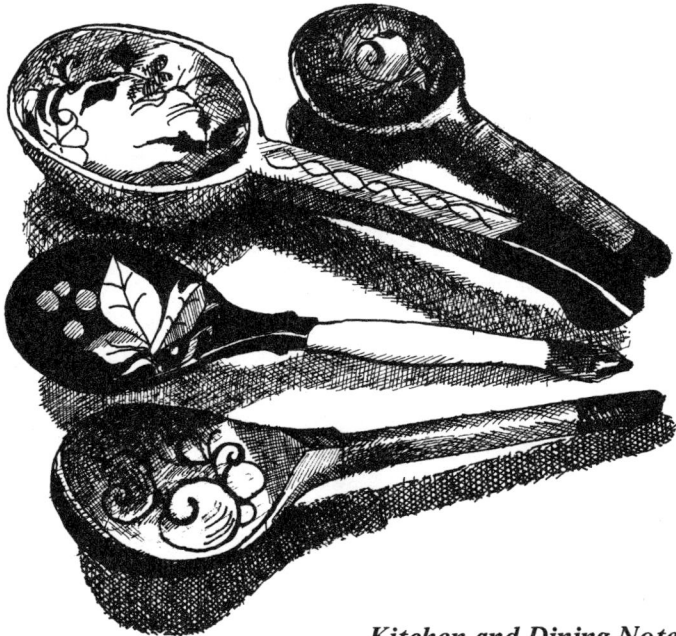

Cutlery

I have two sets of cutlery, a plain, slim, stainless steel set I got nineteen years ago when I got married and a brown handled set with pistol grip knives. After four years of being washed in a dishwasher, the wooden handled ones are beginning to crack. This annoys me because they were fairly expensive and I wanted them to last a long time. If I were to buy silverware again, I'd pick something without special handles.

Serving Pieces

Wooden bowls, baskets, pots and handmade pottery are my favorite serving pieces. I like things that are pleasing in color and texture.

The Dining Room

I don't like to eat in the kitchen. I prefer eating in a room that is free of kitchen clutter, where my eyes are free to appreciate artwork, plants, a pleasing view, or hopefully, all three.

Center Pieces

I think these are silly formalities since they take up prime space for serving and block eye contact. They can always be put on the table and removed when food is served, but that's a bit too contrived for me. I prefer making the dining room itself visually interesting.

Music

People have become so accustomed to Muzak that they surround themselves with background music constantly. I never play music when guests come. I prefer to talk without a background of sound. I do however play music when I am working in the kitchen. It clears my mind and helps relieve any pressure I might feel. Most frequently, I play Bach or Vivaldi.

Flowers

I adore fresh flowers inside the house or outside. As part of housekeeping, in almost every room, I try to have flowers in vases, pitchers and baskets. When we are having guests who stay overnight or longer, I try to remember to place fresh flowers in their rooms to say, "Welcome." Snapdragons, mums and zinnias last longest, but all flowers except oriental poppies last at least a couple of days. When the fresh flowers from the garden are gone, I substitute green plants, dried flowers and the bright colored Mexican crepe-paper flowers.

The Kitchen

I've had seven kitchens during our marriage and am already making plans for my eighth. A kitchen must function well. Doors should open wide enough to give a clear view of what is inside the cabinets. There should be many open shelves. Utensils and equipment should be placed where they are used most frequently. There should be many electrical outlets. Sinks should be deep for minimal splashing. Counters should be at different heights for different chores and should have a generous overhang so that it's easy to scrape off food. At least one counter should be on wheels.

Pots should have heavy bottoms to distribute heat evenly. Most of my pots are Farberware stainless steel with aluminum clad bottoms. I've had them for 19 years. They provide even heat, clean beautifully and look as good now as when I first got them.

If you can manage it, it's nice to have desk space in the kitchen for looking through cookbooks, planning menus, making shopping lists and taking phone messages.

At our Trumansburg farm, I redid the entire kitchen, with oak floors, cabinets with touch latches, maple chopping block counters and 16 feet of a 6 foot high window looking out to the woods. It was a visual joy and very efficient to work in.

Moog suggested that I put one of the counters on wheels so that I could use it in another part of the kitchen or dining room if I needed it. It turned out to be extremely convenient. I used it often as a buffet for moveable feasts. In my next kitchen, I will have one or more counters just like it.

The only change I would make now in that Trumansburg kitchen would be to remove the doors from the eye level cabinets so that the contents are visible. Open shelves like this would eliminate several gestures - - opening the cabinet doors and shutting them.

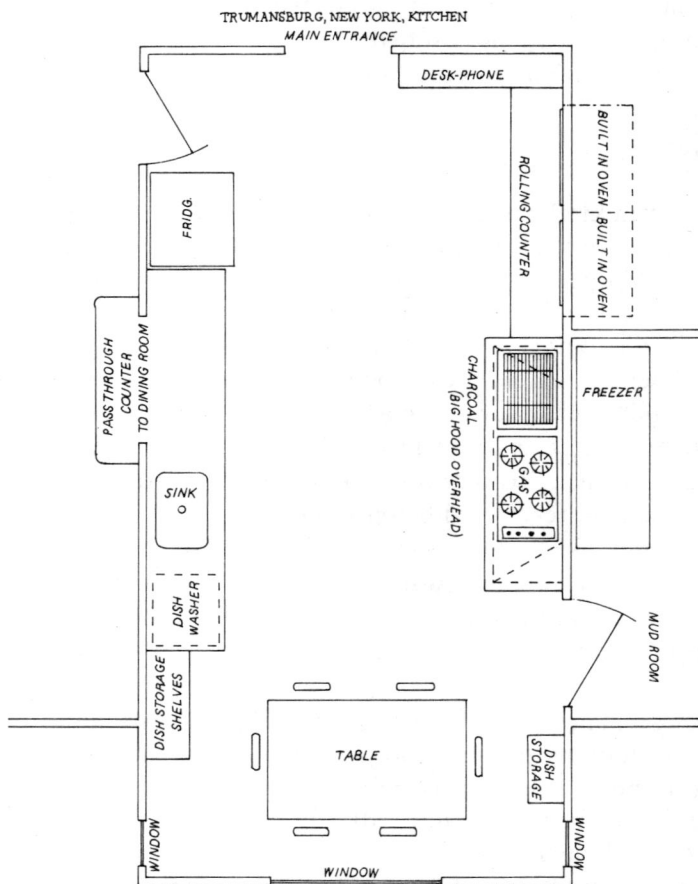

TRUMANSBURG, NEW YORK, KITCHEN

In 1978, we will move to the mountains of North Carolina and I will have the chance to design my first kitchen from the ground up. We are building our own house there, our first house from scratch.

I love natural building materials. The kitchen will have oak floors, poplar cabinets and walnut counters. There will be huge windows and hooks for hanging plants from the ceiling. There will be art prints hung away from the grease of the kitchen stove.

We won't eat in the kitchen - - it will be strictly a work area, with open shelves and a bright yellow pegboard on which to hang pots, pans and utensils.

The cabinets under the counter will have deep, slide-out shelves. Cabinet shelves will be adjustable vertically. The preparation area will be surrounded with open shelves for spices, oils, grains and preparation tools (spoons, spatulas, whisks, etc.) A long magnetic strip for holding knives will be useful on the wall. There will be a desk at the end of one of the counters and an unheated pantry nearby for food storage, canning supplies and a large freezer.

The sink and refrigerator will be restaurant equipment, large and built to last. Anyone setting up a new kitchen should consider restaurant equipment. They are built for function and endurance. I did consider getting a woodburning cookstove but decided not to in the end, because it would be too time consuming and also risky - - an electric or gas stove produces uniform results, whereas a woodburning cookstove does not. I decided on a stove with gas burners and two built–in electric ovens. I like the immediate response of a gas flame and have noticed that electric ovens produce juicier meats than gas ovens. I also decided on a small wood stove for heating the kitchen and to occasionally use for cooking when I have the time to spare.

Last but not least in importance: in my kitchen there will be a tape deck and a radio. Music soothes the most harried cook.

BRIAR COVE, NORTH CAROLINA, KITCHEN

1. There will be open shelves above the counter next to the refrigerator to a height of six feet. Above that, there will be closed storage cabinets.

2. Open shelves or pegboard (hanging area) above the sink and dishwasher to a height of five feet. This is a divider wall and does not go up to the ceiling. There will be 13 1/2 feet of open shelves and 15 feet of wooden chopping block counters.

3. Under counters will be slide-out shelves and vertical cabinets for cookie tins, muffin tins, roasting pans, etc.

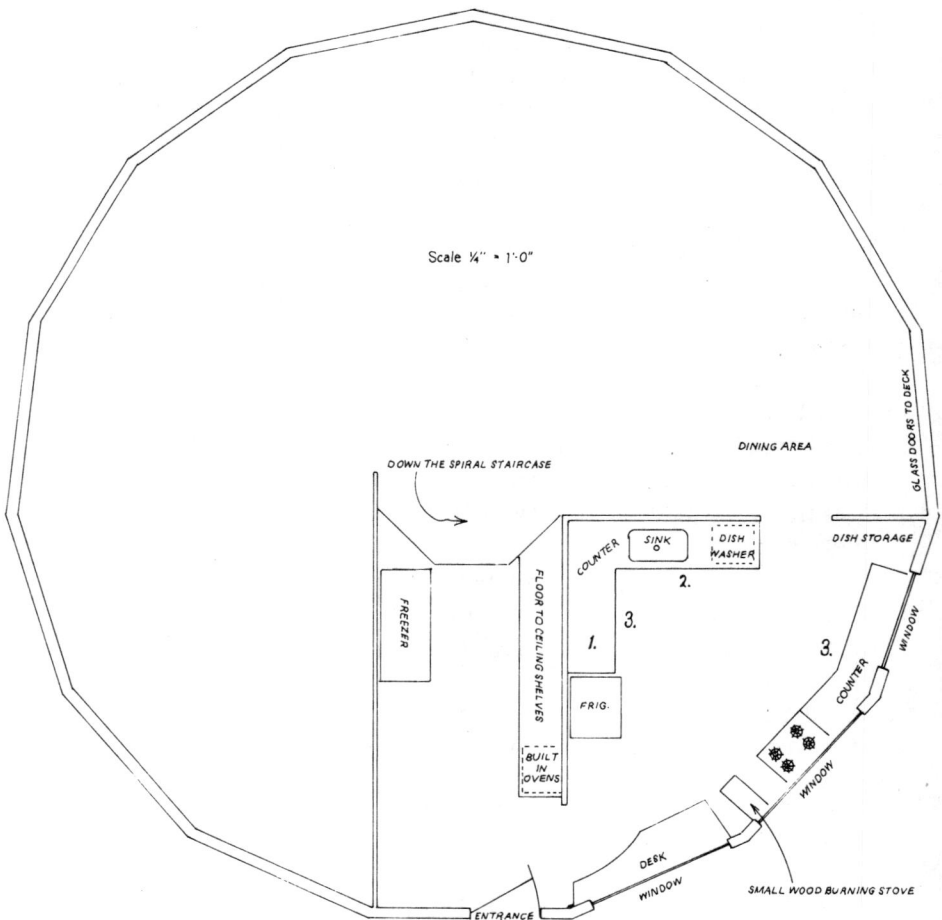

Scale ¼" = 1'-0"

DOWN THE SPIRAL STAIRCASE

DINING AREA

GLASS DOORS TO DECK

FREEZER

FLOOR TO CEILING SHELVES

COUNTER

SINK

DISH WASHER

DISH STORAGE

2.

1.

3.

3.

COUNTER

WINDOW

FRIG.

WINDOW

BUILT IN OVENS

DESK

WINDOW

SMALL WOOD BURNING STOVE

ENTRANCE

16/Kitchen and Dining Notes

Menu Planning & Menus

Menu Planning & Menus

There are many considerations which contribute to the smooth execution of a good dinner. Careful planning will help relax you and your guests. Here are some questions I ask myself before beginning to cook—they may prove useful to you too.

1. *HOW MANY PEOPLE ARE COMING?* If there will be more than 6 or 8 people at the table, it is best to choose a menu which does not require a lot of last minute preparation or you will be driven ragged. Probably the best dish for 9 or more guests is a dish that can be prepared in advance and placed in the oven before the meal. It's reasonable to excuse yourself 15 minutes before dinner in order to put the finishing touches on a meal. If you need more time than this, your planning is most likely at fault.

2. *HAVE YOU ENTERTAINED THESE PEOPLE BEFORE? DO THEY HAVE SPECIAL TASTES?* It pleases people to be remembered as individuals. It's devestating to prepare a main dish some of your guests will not like or to cook an enormous rib roast for vegetarians. Try to remember what your guests have liked in the past. If you have never entertained them before, choose a non—meat meal that your family and friends have enjoyed. You can't go wrong with a meatless meal for a first—time guest. If the majority of your guests are meat—eaters and only 1 or 2 of them are vegetarians, please make sure the vegetarians will have enough to eat—prepare enough side dishes and salad so that they will not leave the table hungry.

3. *WHAT CAN I AFFORD TO BUY? WHAT DO I HAVE ON HAND (IN THE HOUSE) TO WORK WITH?* Once you have decided on the budget—the figure may be increased if you have some ingredients or dishes already stored in the house—you are ready to make up a shopping list and a menu.

**4. *IS THE MEAL VARIED IN TASTE AND TEXTURE?
IS IT A PLEASURE TO PROCEED FROM ONE COURSE
TO ANOTHER?*** Run through the meal you have planned
mentally. Does it give you pleasure? If there is something
wrong, say a repetition of sauced foods or fried foods, then
correct it now. If everything is soft in texture, correct it now.

**5. *HOW CAN I PREPARE IN ADVANCE FOR THE MEAL
I HAVE PLANNED? WHAT SERVING DISHES, POTS,
PLATES, TABLEWARE WILL I BE USING? WHAT WILL
THE TABLE LOOK LIKE?*** Here are some suggestions for
menus appropriate for 6—8 people (formal), 6—10 people
(informal), summer meals and buffets for 6—10 people,
buffets for large groups, and so on. I hope they will prove
helpful.

Sit Down Meals, 3-10 People
Breakfasts

In the old days, hard working farm families ate hearty breakfasts, often ranging from steak to pie. Certainly it is healthful, whenever possible, to begin the day with a stick—to—the—ribs meal which can be worked off the rest of the day.

We enjoy inviting people for Sunday brunch which usually is a festive occasion. All other mornings in the week are rushed—on Sundays we can enjoy a good meal and relaxing time with family and friends.

One of our favorite brunches is pork spareribs with curried fruit. We also enjoy waffles, sausage, smoked fish, omelettes, and yeast breads. You can always strive for a lighter evening meal which can balance out the calorie count.

1. Here is a wonderful, everyday breakfast for your family. It is also good for a guest who has to rush to make a plane.

Fruit in Season
Open Faced Melted Cheese Sandwiches, page 93
Coffee

2. Here are several suggestions for warmed up breakfasts. These leftovers from the night before are good ways to waken the palate—a welcome change from scrambled eggs and bacon.

Blintzes, Spinach Pie, Quiche, Hot Turkey Salad, Souffles, Meat Pie Yannina, Manicotti in Crepe Covers.

See Index, page 209 for page numbers.

The following five breakfasts are for Sundays and holidays, times when you are not rushed and have time to prepare more elaborate meals.

3. Fresh Orange Juice
   Apple Sausage Popover, page 76
   Herb Tea

4. Applesauce, 198
   Bread Pudding with Cream or Milk, 184
   Tea

5. Rhubarb & Cream, 195
   Cottage Cheese Pancakes, 91
   Port Wine Jelly, 143
   Tea

6. Freshly Squeezed Juice
   Apple Raisin Crepes, 200
   Poor Man's Cake, 173
   Tea

7. Grapefruit Half
   Onion, Pepper & Cheese Omelette, 90, with
   Tomato Sauce, 106
   Homemade Muffins, 132
   Coffee

8. While in Munich, we attended the opera and so enjoyed
the mixture of champagne and orange juice we were served
there, that we have it frequently now on gala occasions.

   Fresh Orange Juice with Champagne
   Cheese Blintzes, 86, with Sour Cream &
   Freezer Strawberry Jam, 144
   Coffee with Whipped Cream, 190

Informal Meals, 6-10 People

The main courses here are not gourmet fare—they are just tasty home cooking.

1. Fish Chowder, 102
   Tossed Salad, 126
   Bran Muffins, 134
   Sherried Cheese Spread, 145
   Fruits & Nuts

2. Turkey Soup, 68, with grated cheese
   Wheat Rolls, 135
   Tomato Jam, 142
   Fruit
   Sour Cream Raisin Fudge, 194

3. Chicken & Cornmeal Italienne, 62
   Tossed Salad, 126
   Villa Banfi Red Wine
   Fruit & Cookies

4. Hot Turkey Salad, 67
   Tossed Green Salad, 126
   Corn Bread, 131

5. Tangy Creamed Turkey, 66
   Onion Patch Pudding, 111
   Green Salad with House Dressing, 127
   Coffee Custard, 183
   Whipped Cream, 190
   Coffee

6. Stuffed Cabbage Rolls, 78
   Brown Rice, 112
   Raw Vegetable Tray with Mayonnaise, 128
   Vanilla Ice Cream
   Butterscotch Sauce, 185
   Coffee

7. Grandpa's Favorite Chicken Stew, 58
   Tossed Salad, 126
   Apple Raisin Nut Crepe, 200
   Herb Tea

8. Swedish Meatballs, 71
   Spaetzle, 109
   Green Salad, 126
   House Dressing, 127
   Fresh Apple Cake, 168
   Cream Cheese Frosting, 169
   Herb Tea

9. Italian Meatballs, 72
   Stir Fry Vegetables, 114
   Garlic Bread, 140
   Brandied Fruit, 186
   Whipped Cream, 190
   Coffee

Formal Meals, 6-8 People

1. Veal Milanese, 83
   String Beans in Lemon Butter with Toasted Almonds, 118
   Noodles al Pesto, 104
   Celery Olive Salad, 125
   Soave Wine
   Zabaglione, 180
   Whipped Cream, 190
   Demi-tasse

2. Roasted Cornish Game Hen, 64
   Carrot Radish Salad, 124
   Broccoli with Cheese Sauce, 117
   Chablis Wine
   Tosca Cake, 160
   Tea

3. Greek Spinach Pie, 94
   Tossed Salad, 126
   Herb Bread, 139
   Greek Olives
   Cambas Roditys Rose Wine
   Baklava, 174
   Tea

4. Herbed Goulash, 80
   Spinach Salad, 122
   Spaetzle, 109
   Christian Bros. Barbera Wine
   Molasses Ice Cream, 193
   Coffee

5. Chicken Paprika, 55
   Radish Salad, 123
   Spaetzle, 109
   Sebastiani Green Hungarian Dry Wine
   Walnut Torte, 156
   Coffee

6. Oriental Beef & Carrots, 81
   Stir Fry Vegetables, 114
   Brown Rice with Sauteed Mushrooms, 112
   Villa Banfi Roman White Wine
   Lace Wafers, 178
   Tea

7. Crab Stuffed Mushrooms, 98
   Tossed Salad, 126, or Spinach Salad, 122
   Cheese Bread, 138, with Tomato Jam, 142
   K. Franck Johannesburg Riesling Wine
   Cheesecake, 152
   Coffee

8. Manicotti in Crepe Covers, 85
   Spinach Salad, 122
   Herb Bread, 139
   Ruffino Chianti Wine
   Custard Marmalade Rum Cake, 158
   Coffee

9. Spaghetti with White Clam Sauce, 103
   Sausage Stuffed Mushrooms, 74
   Salad Tray with Celery, Carrots, Green & Black Olives
   Garlic Bread,140
   Villa Banfi Red Wine
   Vanilla Ice Cream with Nesselrode Sauce, 189
   Coffee or Tea

10. Veal Dagmar, 84
    Green Salad with House Dressing, 127
    Spaetzle, 109
    Pound Cake, 172, with Mocha Frosting
    Coffee

Summer Meals & Buffets, 6-10 People

In the summer, light meals with cool courses and desserts are what most people favor. Most of the following meals keep cooking to a minimum.

1. Gazpacho, 96, with garnishes
   Cheese Tray
   Fruit & Cookies
   Sangria, 205

2. Carrot Tuna Salad, 124
   Wheat Rolls, 135
   Garbanzo Spread, 147
   Wine Cooler, 207
   Lemon Ice Milk, 191
   Date Nut Bars, 177

3. Cracked Wheat Salad, 122
   Quiche, 88
   Herb Bread, 139
   Cold Rose Wine
   Apricot Souffle, 182

4. Tuna Souffle, 101
   Spinach Salad, 122
   Wheat Rolls, 135
   Tomato Jam, 142
   Rhubarb & Heavy Cream, 195

5. Tossed Salad, 126, with Cheese or Meat Strips
   Popovers, 137
   Port Wine Jelly, 143
   Iced Tea
   Cold Cantaloupe with Lemon Wedge
   Brandy Balls, 194

6. Skirt Steak Roulades, 82
   Feta Cheese Salad, 121
   Garlic Bread, 140
   Red Wine Cooler, 207
   Honey Almond Parfait, 190

7. Cheese Omelette, 90
   Cold Ratatouille, 119
   Herb Bread, 139
   Wine Cooler, 207
   Molasses Ice Cream, 193

8. Raw Vegetable Platter
   Garbanzo Dip, 147, & Yogurt Tahini Dip, 147
   Wheat Rolls, 135, & Butter
   Port Wine Jelly, 143
   Iced Herb Tea
   Fresh Fruit
   Cream Cheese Coffee Cake, 171

9. Raw Vegetable Platter with Curried Mayonnaise, 128
   Cheese Tray
   Bread & Crackers
   Fresh Fruit
   Nuts

10. Salad Bar
    Cheese Bread, 138
    Pepper Jam, 144
    Mint Tea with Lemon
    Cold Watermelon

Some Special Meals, 3-6 People

SIX HOUR ITALIAN DINNER (FOR 3–4)

Our first visit to Rome was a truly joyous occasion. Many of our friends had told us about the beauty of the city, the inexpensive and exquisite food, and the relaxed atmosphere. When we arrived, we had many friends who wanted to show us the sights and take us to all the good eating places.

We spent many evenings going to dinner at 8 and enjoying the conversation and food right up to closing time. The clock, when we finally looked at it, usually read well after midnight!

Back in the states we remembered this style and pace of eating. When we heard that one of our best friends was coming to visit, we decided to recreate for him one of our leisurely Roman meals.

The menu which follows, though extensive, is easy to prepare. All but the two main courses may be prepared ahead of time. Moog and I each prepared one dish so that our guest was never alone. The meal started at 6 P.M. and ended a bit after midnight. No one was stuffed. We all enjoyed an evening of carefully chosen, well cooked food and flowing conversation.

I don't think you can do this kind of thing with more than two couples. It requires people who listen to each other rather than cross talk. (This can occur even with four people, if they are the wrong four.) It also requires people who love eating and drinking in a leisurely manner.

Antipasto with Dry Sherry
Garlic Bread, 140
Fusilli with Fresh Grated Romano Cheese, 105
Veal Milanese with Lemon Slices, 83, with Dry White Wine
Prosciutto Wrapped Pears with Torrone
Demi-tasse, Cannoli & Cognac

For the antipasto, arrange these ingredients attractively on a bed
of lettuce:

> fennel or celery with olive salt
> Italian salami
> pickled peppers
> artichoke hearts in oil
> caponata (eggplant relish)
> Greek olives, black & green
> pickled mushrooms
> radishes

In Rome, when finocchio or fennel is ordered, the waiter takes
the olive oil cruet and pours about 1/4 cup of it into a shallow
bowl. Then he pours enough salt into the oil to layer the bottom
of the bowl lightly. The waiter mixes the mixture carefully. As
you eat the fennel, you dip it into the mixture of oil and salt
which is called, appropriately enough, olive salt.

The second course is the pasta. I used fusilli which is a curly
type of spaghetti. Cook it according to directions and serve it
with a sauce containing tomatoes, onions, anchovies, cauliflower,
pine nuts, currants and salt and pepper. See page 105 for details.

For the first dessert, the wrapped pears, core the pears and cut
them into 6 pieces. Torrone is a nougat candy with almonds in
the center, flavored with vanilla, lemon or orange.

Moog and I served the dinner this way. We ate the antipasto on
the coffee table. While we were talking, Moog got up and prepared
the fusilli. When it was ready, we went to the dining room table
and ate it. Talking and laughing, we went back to the couch. Then
I left to prepare the veal. When it was ready, we went back to the
table. After about 30 minutes, we had the pears, prosciutto and
torrone and nibbled awhile. About 11:30 P.M., I made demi-tasse
and served the cannoli. Shortly before midnight, we enjoyed a
nightcap of cognac.

Sweet dreams were had by all.

GUINEA HEN FOR 6

One weekend my two in-laws and the principals from an earlier Synthesizer record were at the house. Since my mother-in-law loves formality, the occasion was ripe for a small-size bash.

Roasted Game Hens, 64   (Half a bird for each person)
String Beans in Lemon Butter, 118
Tossed Green Salad, 126
Popovers, 137
Dry White Wine
Walnut Torte, 156
Coffee

This is really a simple meal to prepare. I made the cake in the morning, then the stuffing for the hens which ships up pretty fast. I made the salad, but did not add the artichoke hearts or dressing. I saved these for the last minute before serving at table. I stored the salad in the refrigerator til dinner time.

A bit after we had cocktails, I excused myself and popped the hens into the oven. I then mixed up the popovers and melted the butter in the muffin pans. In one hour, both the hens and the popovers would be ready. The only item left to do was to pop the previously cleaned beans into the steamer. The lemon butter was in a jar in the refrigerator. I quickly toasted the almonds, left them on the stove to keep warm and came back to my guests.

One of my children took care of the string beans while I was with my guests. This was one meal where the children were not present. They were old enough to make themselves a sandwich and pour a glass of milk. I promised them I'd save some cake.

Menus For Large Groups of People, 10-100

These menus require a minimum of fussing considering the quantity of people. All the desserts and baking can be done ahead of time and can be frozen or refrigerated.

Buffet Dinners, 10-30 People

1. This is the least fussy menu on this page. The caramel custard calls for a bit of finesse. The rest is straightforward.

Chicken in Lemon Caper Butter, 56
Tossed Salad, 126
Brown Rice, 112
Chablis Blanc
Caramel Custard, 181
Butter Cookies

2. The meat pie requires pie crust preparation and mixing of meat, cheese, eggs, etc. for the filling, but the taste is worth the effort.

Meat Pie Yannina, 77
Feta Cheese Salad, 121
Herb Bread, 139
Greek Red Wine
Biscuit Tortoni, 191
Demi-tasse

3. The meatballs in this menu require forming by hand.
This can be time consuming if you are serving a large number
of people.

Kufte, 70, or Cumin Meatballs, 73
Kasha Varnishkes, 110
Dilled Carrots in Orange Butter, 118
Christian Brothers Barbera Wine
Apricot Souffle, 182
Lace Wafers, 178
Herb Tea

4. The chicken must be browned and the curry sauce made,
but neither takes very long.

Apple Curried Chicken, 60
Brown Rice, 112
Grated Carrot Salad, 124
Orange Ice Cream, 192
Butter Cookies
Mint Tea

5. Nothing here takes much time to do except for boning
the turkey and chopping the ingredients for the Hot
Turkey Salad.

Hot Turkey Salad, 67
Spinach Salad, 122
Curried Fruit, 120
Cheese Bread, 138
Chablis Blanc
Gelatin Dessert, 196
Date Nut Bars, 177
Tea

Vegetarian Buffets, 10-30 People

Most people think of vegetarian food as unappetizing but good for you.These dishes are appetizing *and* good for you.

1. Spinach Egg Cheese Bake,97
   Brown Rice with Sauteed Onions & Mushrooms, 112
   Cole Slaw, 125
   Bran Muffins, 134
   Tomato Ginger Jam, 142
   Peaches & Cream Cheesecake, 170
   Coffee

2. Stuffed Cheese Tufoli, 75, with Tomato Sauce, 106
   Tossed Salad, 126, with House Dressing, 127
   Garlic Bread, 140
   Zabaglione Rum Cake,158
   Demi-tasse

3. Sprout Fu Yong, 100
   Brown Rice with Sauteed Onions & Mushrooms, 112
   Stir Fry Vegetables, 114
   Fresh Fruit
   Lace Wafers, 178, or Butter Cookies

4. Eggplant Manicotti, 92
   Green Salad, 126, with Green Mayonnaise, 128
   Herb Bread, 139
   Mocha Cream Pie, 151
   Red Zinger Tea with Honey

5. Quiche, 88
   Spinach Salad, 122
   Bran Muffins, 134
   White Wine
   Marron Glace with Vanilla Ice Cream, 188
   Herb Tea

Bread, Cheese & Wine Party, 16-25 People

This is one of the easiest parties we've ever given. It is grand in the summer when you pick your own vegetables. Each of the guests brought two loaves of homemade bread. We provided:

Cheese
Butter
Fresh Vegetables on a Platter with Various Dips
Marmite
Tomato Jam
Port Wine Jelly
Wine
Fruit
Homemade Cookies

We were fortunate to live near the Cornell Dairy Store. As I recall, we had 5 lbs. of New York State sharp cheddar, a few lbs. of smoked Gouda that we have never found any-where else, a caraway studded Danish farmers' cheese with taste and texture like brick cheese, a caramel colored goat cheese, Kings Choice Port Salut, and real cream cheese. All the cheeses were at room temperature where they taste best. I set up the dining room with cutting boards and sharp knives for cutting the cheese and bread, plates for the cheese, and knives for the butter and jam. Fresh vegetables abounded on large platters. I had a center piece of whole vegetables in a big woven basket. Glasses were needed for the Almaden Mountain Red and Gallo Chablis Blanc. A rustic handwoven cloth and flowered napkins completed the scene.

Come By For A Drink,
Any Number Of People

This may be another name for a cocktail party or a casual way
of inviting friends over.

Sangria, 205
Wine Punch, 206, or Jug Wine
Juice & Soda
Rumaki, 50
Artichokes Wrapped in Bacon, 49
Chili Con Queso & Corn Chips, 148
Raw Vegetable Tray and 3 Dips
Meat Pie Yannina, 77
Cocktail Rye Bread with Sherried Cheese Spread, 145, & Marmite
Marinated Mushrooms, 50
Cheese Wedges & Crackers
Biscuit Tortoni, 191
Coffee or Tea

4 or 7 days before the party you should:

1. make your shopping list and buy what you need
2. plan the dishes, cloths and table settings you will use
3. make the Marinated Mushrooms
4. make the juice or fruit cubes for punch (the larger you make them the longer they will last)

2 or 3 days before the party:

1. make Sherried Cheese Spread
2. make Chili Con Queso (only up to step 5)

Morning before the party:

1. prepare the Raw Vegetable Tray with the Dips
2. make the Artichokes Wrapped in Bacon and Rumaki but don't bake
3. get out the dishes, glasses, silverware, etc.
4. prepare Meat Pie Yannina but don't put filling in crust until you are ready to bake

1 hour before party:

1. put the Meat Pie in oven
2. assemble materials for drinks
3. warm the Chili Con Queso
4. cook the Artichokes Wrapped in Bacon and Rumaki
5. set out the platters of Vegetables, Cheeses, and Bread

1/2 hour before party:

1. make the Sangria and Wine Punch

And please remember to take a nap in the afternoon.

A Dinner For 25

When we first moved to Buffalo, John Eaton, the composer, came to visit. He had many friends at SUNY at Buffalo, so we decided to have a party for him. He met a lot of his old acquaintances and we made a lot of new friends.

Crab Stuffed Mushrooms, 98
Rumaki, 50
Artichoke Hearts Wrapped In Bacon, 49
Manicotti, 85
Tossed Salad, 126
Garlic Bread, 140
Ruffino Chianti
Biscuit Tortoni, 191
Demi-tasse

This is an ideal way to feed a large crowd. The hot hors d'oeuvres are passed before dinner. The Manicotti are easy to serve and don't drip. Salad and Garlic Bread are easy for people to serve themselves. Tortoni comes in a disposable cup.

Easy & Inexpensive Buffets, 35-40 People

Our first summer in business, Moog decided he would set up many small studios and have people from all over the U.S. come to our shop and use them. He sent out notices and soon the responses came rolling in. He requested three things of me:

1. that I find temporary housing for the participants and their families at the price they wanted to pay

2. that I have a few people in for every meal for the three weeks of the seminar so that they would feel welcome

3. that I make one large dinner each week for everyone.

This was 1965; we had two children and we were living on a food budget of $35 a month. We had no dishwasher. It turned out I had to make only two large dinners—one of the wives of the participants, a very gracious lady, volunteered to take over the third meal.

My husband paid for someone to take care of the children. Friends generously left me bags of vegetables from their garden. Some of the more settled participants gave parties to which we were invited, which alleviated some of the pressure I was under. Everything went off very well. Here are the two menus I used which fed 35—40 people most inexpensively.

A Welcome Dinner

25 lb. Turkey, roasted
Macaroni Salad
Raw Vegetable Tray with Sour Cream Dip
Wine Punch
Watermelon
2 Large Sheet Cakes (1 Chocolate and 1 Lemon)

BYOB Dinner

Barbequed Chicken
Assorted Salads
Bran Muffins
Fresh Fruit
Doughnuts

Many people brought jugs of wine to the BYOB dinner and
were nice enough to leave half-full jugs when they left. This
made the everyday entertaining of participants in the seminars
easier for me.

A Cookout Brunch, 40-50 People

We really enjoy cookouts. Whether it is the first beautiful spring weekend, our anniversary, or just an excuse for a party, the combination of eating, cooking and enjoying the outdoors has a real celebration of life feeling.

One day we invited our friends for a day long party with the understanding that we would provide the brunch and drinks, and they would bring a dish to pass for the evening meal. It was a glorious day of games, swimming and talking. At least fifteen families enjoyed it with us. After dinner, we made a tremendous bonfire.

Since all the plates and cups were made of paper, it took us only an hour or two to clean up the next day, a simple expenditure of time for such a wonderful day's worth of entertaining.

I particularly enjoy these cookouts because I can do all the indoor cooking ahead of time and leave the outdoor cooking to Moog.

Beer
Orange Juice
Hamburgers or Polish Sausage
Tons of Scrambled Eggs (usually fried in bacon fat)
Bread, Rolls, Bagels, Muffins, etc.
Coffee Cakes and Cookies
Coffee

For the evening meal we supplied cold wine, wine coolers, Sangria, beer, lemonade, iced tea and soda. It's important to have plenty of cold drinks available in the afternoon and evening—children especially get very thirsty.

Be sure you have enough cold storage space (an extra refrigerator in a friend's house is fine) for the goodies.

A Buffet For 100 People

One summer in the late 60's, Moog decided to have a small weekend seminar. That was when John Eaton was composer in residence at the studio. Moog, John, and Joel Chadabe were each to give a half day presentation on their special concerns in electronic music.

We were in the process of remodeling our farmhouse and the house was stripped down to brick walls and sub-flooring. Moog asked me to give a cocktail party for 10–15 people. I said I'd be glad to if he didn't mind the funky decor. I needn't have worried. The fifteen people grew to a hundred and we had to hire the floor of the Masonic Temple in downtown Trumansburg.

Our business manager thought it would be very classy to have a House Beautiful type of buffet—turkeys with paper curls on their legs, hams decorated with pineapple and cherries, so on. The catch was that he was willing to part with only $100 to do it. To placate him, I called up various ladies' clubs and caterers to see what this kind of meal would cost. The lowest price I found was $3–$4 per person for a roast beef and canned vegetable dinner.

When I reported these figures to our manager and he had recovered, I told him I could do the job for $100, but he would have to settle for something more earthy than his original dream. I had no time for an elaborate buffet—I was much too busy. I had three children, the youngest just nine months old, and moreover was payroll bookkeeper for our company of 40 employees. But I had fed many an artist and musician by then and knew what kind of food they liked and I knew they would enjoy the simple menu I had in my mind. The business manager acquiesced to my proposal, but only because my price was right.

My considerations for the party were as follows: I was dealing with people I didn't know and had better choose good, common denominator food. Since many musicians tend to be vegetarians, I would have to see to it they had a good meal too. And, finally, since I was working by myself, I'd best keep things simple. This was the menu that evolved.

Good Bread
Cold Meats
Cheese
Trays of Cold Sliced Raw Vegetables
Relishes
Beverages
Dessert

Good Bread—We had a very good bakery that made all kinds of
solid, tasty bread. I bought two huge round sour ryes, two
black Russian pumpernickels, three or four challahs (soft egg
bread), three dozen onion pockets (rectangular onion rolls which
were a bakery specialty—the insides were loaded with chopped
onion) and three dozen hard rolls. I had the rye and pumpernickel sliced and wrapped them securely in double plastic bags
to keep them from drying out and stored them in my freezer.
All the other bread and rolls I froze whole and sliced on the day
of the buffet.

Cold Meats—I bought lean canned ham, bologna and salami,
25—30 lbs. worth. I arrived at this amount by asking the butcher
a standard way of figuring the correct amount of meat for two
sandwiches of meat with lettuce and/or cheese. He suggested
1/4 lb. of meat for each person. By purchasing 5 lbs. extra, I
gave myself a leeway of 40 extra sandwiches for very hungry
people who might eat more than two sandwiches apiece. The
butcher was very kind and sliced, wrapped and stored the meat
until the day I needed it.

Cheese—I went to Cornell at the beginning of the week and
purchased two 5 lb. wheels of New York State Sharp Cheddar
and 10 lbs. of sliced imported Swiss cheese.

Trays of Cold Sliced Raw Vegetables—I cleaned these, sliced
them, and soaked them in cold water a couple of days—carrots,
celery, radishes and cauliflower. On the day of the buffet, I
sliced raw green and yellow squash, cucumbers and peppers.
I opened jars of green and black olives. I chose not to serve
tomatoes since they are messy to handle and I didn't want to
use forks at table. I put together big bowls of garden and ice-
berg lettuce of proper size for sandwiches. Most of the vegetables were from our garden or our friends'. I arranged all

vegetables attractively on large platters with bowls of mayonnaise set in the center.

Relishes—I toted up from the basement jars of homemade pickles (green tomato, zucchini, and bread and butter pickles) and dinner jams (port wine, tomato and mint). I provided mustard, mayonnaise and butter.

Beverages—I decided on Almaden Rose as a nice middle of the road wine. I chilled eight gallons. I made the same amount of fresh lemonade. I was lucky in that the Masonic Temple had huge refrigerators.

Dessert—I skimmed by with bowls of after dinner mints, the kind everyone likes and takes in handfuls from restaurants— they have centers of colored jelly.

On the day of the seminar, I had everything on platters, ready to go. While the seminar was going on, I worked quietly in the kitchen. Once the seminar was over, I had just one hour to get the buffet set up. Moog and the business manager helped move chairs and tables.

The Tables—I used tablecloths and utensils from the Temple but bought candles out of my budget of $100. Flowers were donated by local restaurants and motels who were grateful for the extra business the seminar was making for them. I used sturdy paper plates, cups and napkins.

I set two eighteen foot long tables with platters that were duplicated six times. Every six feet there was a repeat setting of everything available. The tables could be approached from either side in order to serve as many guests at one time as possible.

I stationed myself at one table to pour wine or lemonade and Moog and the business manager took the other table. It took a bit of hustling, but before I knew it, everyone was eating and talking and congratulating me on the "great food." The young people and the older people, the vegetarians and the meat eaters were all happy. That even included our business manager.

The baby sitter brought our three girls over to the buffet. They enjoyed the attention they were given. I basked quietly in the knowledge that I had pulled it off.

The leftovers from the buffet were very useful the next week. They enabled me to take it easy and recuperate.

There is a funny end to the story of this buffet. After it was all over, I dragged myself home, preparing to hibernate for a day or two. No sooner had I hit the sack when Moog called to say that a friend had just arrived in town with a rich acquaintance who was interested in investing in our business. They wanted to take us to dinner in a couple of hours. Could I be ready? I called a friend with babysitting daughters and asked if one of them could come over immediately. She came and took over completely.

I took a shower, washed my hair, towel dried it, manicured my nails, shaved my legs, and flopped down to rest for a half hour. I just finished getting dressed when it was time to go. The two visitors who didn't know what I'd been up to that day commented on how rested and lovely I looked. When the spirit is willing, anything is possible.

Hors D'Oeuvres

Hors D'Oeuvres

† *Easy recipes for the inexperienced hostess.*

Main Courses Served As Hors D'Oeuvres

When I work hard to prepare a good meal, the last thing I want to do is ruin appetites by serving filling hors d'oeuvres. If I serve them at all, they are light and teasing to the palate, rather than heavy and cumbersome. I usually serve simple things like a wedge of cheese or unsalted cashews.

When the meal is a buffet, where variety of dishes adds to the effect or, when I am planning a late or light meal, I serve appetizers.

There are many recipes in this book that can be used as hors d'oeuvres.

Chili Con Queso, 148
Fresh Vegetable Platter & Curried Mayonnaise, 128 or
Chick Pea Dip, 147, or Yogurt Tahini, 147
Quiche, 88
Crab Stuffed Mushrooms, 98
Swedish Meatballs, 71
Italian Meatballs, 72
Meat Pie Yannina, 77
Cumin Meatballs, 73

Artichoke Hearts Wrapped In Bacon

1 box frozen artichoke hearts
1/4 lb bacon

1. Wrap each artichoke heart with half a piece of bacon and secure with a toothpick.
2. Broil slowly until the bacon is cooked. This also cooks the artichoke and gives it a nice bacon flavor.
3. Serve hot and leave the toothpick in for a handle.

Makes about 24

Marinated Mushrooms

Olive oil, vinegar, oregano and garlic make these mushrooms so good you can't eat just one!

> 1 1/2 lbs firm small mushrooms
> 1 1/2 cups water
> 1/2 cup wine vinegar
> 1 cup Italian dressing, see p. 127
> (should include salt,pepper & oregano)

1. Clean and dry the mushrooms.
2. Mix the water and vinegar and heat to a boil. Add the mushrooms and let boil 2 minutes. Drain the liquid and reserve ½ cup of it.
3. Cool the mushrooms in the refrigerator for 1 hour
4. Mix the reserved liquid with the dressing and pour over the cooled mushrooms.

They are ready to eat immediately, but the flavor improves after several hours. They can be kept refrigerated for 1 week to 10 days.

Serves 4-8

Rumaki

> 1 can water chestnuts, drained
> 1/4–1/2 lb bacon
> soy sauce

1. Cut the chestnuts in half and place in a pie plate or large saucer.
2. Pour enough soy sauce in the dish to half cover the chestnuts. Let them soak for about 20 minutes on each side, turning once.
3. Wrap each chestnut half with a piece of bacon and secure with a toothpick.
4. Broil slowly until the bacon is done. Serve hot.

Makes about 24

Cheese & Marmite On Rye Bread

Swiss, colby or brick cheese
Marmite
cocktail rye bread

Spread the small bread slices with a thin layer of Marmite and top with a slice of cheese. Cover with wrap or serve immediately.

Hot Chicken Wings

A Buffalo specialty. Serve these with napkins—they are juicy. And remember to have plenty of cold drinks on hand—these wings are peppery.

2 lbs chicken wings
1/4 cup vinegar
1/2 cup oil
1 large bottle Frank's Hot Sauce (12 oz)

1. Cut wings in half.
2. Marinate 1 hour in vinegar, oil and hot sauce. Remove from marinade and drain.
3. Bake 1 hour 350°.

The hot sauce contains cayenne pepper, vinegar, salt and garlic.

Serves 6

Croque Monsieur

These are French cheese and ham sandwiches, dipped in egg and fried. Cut in quarters, they are delectable appetizers.

10 slices thin sliced wheat bread
5 slices ham or turkey
5 slices Swiss or Mozzarella cheese
fresh ground pepper
pinch allspice
3 eggs, beaten
4 T milk
1/4 lb sweet butter

1. Lightly butter one side of each slice of bread.
2. Place a slice of meat and a slice of cheese on each buttered slice of bread. Repeat for 4 more slices.
3. Season with pepper and allspice.
4. Cover with remaining bread slices, butter side down toward filling.
5. Beat eggs and milk together.
6. Dip each sandwich into the egg mixture and fry in butter until crisply golden on both sides.

Makes 5 sandwiches or 20 appetizers

Main Courses

Main Courses

Poultry

Chicken Paprika /55

‡† Chicken In Lemon Caper Butter /56

Grandpa's Favorite Chicken Stew /58

Apple Curried Chicken /60

Chicken & Cornmeal Italienne /62

‡† Roasted Game Hens /64

Giblet Gravy For Poultry /65

Tangy Creamed Turkey /66

† Hot Turkey Salad /67

Turkey Soup /68

Ground Meat

Lamb & Wheat Meatballs (Kufte) /70

‡† Swedish Meatballs /71

‡† Italian Meatballs /72

‡ Cumin Meatballs /73

Sausage Stuffed Mushrooms /74

† Stuffed Tufoli /75

Apple Sausage Popovers /76

Meat Pie Yannina /77

Stuffed Cabbage Rolls /78

Beef & Veal

‡† Herbed Goulash /80

Oriental Beef & Carrots /81

† Marinated Skirt Steak Roulades /82

† Veal Milanese /83

Veal Dagmar /84

Cheese & Eggs

Manicotti In Crepe Covers /85

‡ Mom's Blintzes /85

Onion Quiche /88

Omelettes /90

Cottage Cheese Pancakes /91

Eggplant Manicotti /92

Open Melted Cheese Sandwiches /93

1-2-3 Buffet /93

Spanakopita (Greek Spinach Pie) /94

Gazpacho /96

† Spinach Egg Cheese Bake /97

Seafood

† Crab Stuffed Mushrooms /98

Crab Fu Yong /100

Tuna Souffle /101

Fish Chowder /102

Pasta

Spaghetti With White Clam Sauce /103

† Genovese Noodles Al Pesto /104

Fusilli With Cauliflower /105

‡ Spaghetti With Tomato Sauce /106

† **Easy recipes for the inexperienced hostess.**

‡ **These recipes can be frozen.**

Poultry
Chicken Paprika

The paprika is the magic in this dish. Make sure it is the best
Hungarian paprika you can get. The sauce is loaded with onions
and paprika and smoothed with sour cream.

> 1/2 stick (2 oz) sweet butter
> 6 medium onions, coarsely cut
> 1 chicken (3–3 1/2 lb) cut into serving size pieces
> 2 T imported Hungarian paprika *
> 1/2–3/4 cup chicken broth
> 1/2–1 cup sour cream, at room temperature

1. Melt the butter in a large kettle. Add the onions and cook
over low heat for about 30 minutes until onions are limp but
not browned. Stir occasionally.
2. Add the chicken pieces, skin side down. Cover, turn up heat
slightly and simmer. When the chicken starts to turn golden,
turn the pieces and cover again. Simmer for 1/2 hour, until
chicken is tender.
3. Remove the kettle from the heat, Sprinkle in the paprika
and mix gently. Simmer for an additional 5 minutes over low
heat. The onions should have the consistency of a puree. If
there doesn't seem to be enough sauce, add the chicken broth
and stir well. Add salt to taste.
4. Cover the kettle and cook another 10 minutes over low heat
until the sauce has thickened. If the sauce is still too thin, cook
without the lid until the liquid has reduced.
5. Just before serving, stir in the sour cream. Heat through
but do not let boil, or the sour cream will curdle.

*If you are not using real Hungarian paprika, reduce the
quantity of paprika slightly. Domestic paprika is sharp rather
than sweet.

Serves 4

Chicken In Lemon Caper Butter

John Cage is probably the most well known composer in avant-garde electronic music. He's always a jump or two ahead of everyone. It's always a treat to talk to him—his wit is low-key and biting. David Tudor has collaborated with John Cage and other electronic music composers.

When Moog first started the business, we pinched every penny. I had a few standard dishes for guests which were tasty and inexpensive. Ordinarily, I would have omitted mushrooms from this specialty of mine, chicken in lemon caper butter, but when I heard that John Cage and David Tudor were coming to dinner, I decided to splurge on fresh mushrooms. They were my first VIP guests, and I was a bit anxious.

When I served the meal, John told me how much he loved mushrooms. I was tickled to have lucked out. This is the recipe I have used most often in entertaining—it's a consistent winner.

> 3 lbs frying chicken, cut into serving pieces
> 1/4 lb butter
> juice and pulp from 2 lemons
> 3 T capers
> 2 cloves garlic, minced
> salt and fresh ground pepper to taste
> 1/2 t imported paprika
> 1 lb mushrooms, sliced

1. Combine all ingredients except chicken and mushrooms in a large skillet or Dutch oven and bring to a boil.
2. Lower the heat and add chicken pieces, skin side down. Continue to cook over low heat for 30—45 minutes, or until chicken is tender.
3. Add mushrooms. Continue basting and cooking for 15 minutes more.

This dish is good served over brown rice or noodles, garnished with parsley. If you need to double this recipe, it is better to use two pots so that the chicken can completely absorb the flavor from the pan juices.

Serves 4

Grandpa's Favorite Chicken Stew

This is a lovely, old fashioned country recipe. The dumplings are the lightest I have ever tasted. If you are going to double the recipe, use two large pots. That way, the chicken will absorb all the flavor from the pan juice and you will have plenty of space to drop the dumplings.

Moog's dad says his mother used to make this dish once a week. Not such a bad idea—it's very good.

> 1 chicken, about 3 lbs, cut into serving pieces
> 3 T butter
> 3 stalks diced celery, including the leaves, minced
> 1 medium onion, chopped
> 1 bay leaf
> 1 t dill or celery salt
> 1/2 t ground pepper
> salt to taste
> 3 cups water
> 3 T flour

1. Brown the chicken in the butter.
2. Add the celery, onion, bay leaf, dill (or celery salt), pepper, salt and water. Bring to a boil and simmer covered for one hour or until chicken is tender.
3. Remove the chicken with a slotted spoon. Thicken the pan juices with the flour blended in a little water and return the chicken to the pot.
4. Drop the dumplings by the teaspoonful onto the chicken pieces. Cover and simmer gently to steam the dumplings. They should be done in about 10 minutes. A toothpick inserted into a dumpling will come out clean when the dumplings are cooked.

DUMPLINGS

I usually make a double batch of these herb dumplings—they have a way of disappearing.

> 7/8 cup flour
> 1 t baking powder
> 1/4 t sage
> 1/4 t thyme
> pinch cumin
> 1/2 t salt
> 1 T oil
> 2 T minced parsley or celery leaves
> 1 egg
> 3 T milk

1. Combine the flour, baking powder, seasonings, oil and parsley in a large mixing bowl.
2. With a fork, beat in the egg and milk.
3. Mix well. Drop by the teaspoonful on top of the chicken pieces. The dumplings should not sit in the sauce while they are cooking.
   These dumplings cannot be frozen.

Serves 4

Apple Curried Chicken

The sauce from this dish is thick, creamy and zesty. It is great served over brown rice, kasha, or spaetzle.

2 chickens (2–3 lb), quartered
1/2 cup flour
1/3 cup salad oil
2 large apples
4 medium onions, sliced
2 t chopped green pepper
1/2 cup celery
1 T butter
2–3 T curry powder
1–2 t salt
1/2 t ground ginger
1/2 cup sour cream or yogurt
2/3 cup unsalted cashews or almonds
2 T chopped mint leaves

1. Coat the chicken with flour.
2. Heat the oil in a 6 quart Dutch oven. Over medium heat, cook the pieces of chicken until browned on all sides. Cook just a few pieces at a time. Set the chicken aside but leave the oil in the pan.
3. Peel, core and chop the apples.
4. Cook the apples, onions, chopped pepper, celery, curry powder, salt and ginger in the same oil that the chicken was cooked in. Cook until the onions are tender, and stir occasionally.
5. Add 1 cup of water to the apple-onion mixture. Put through a blender at high speed until the mixture is smooth.
6. Return the chicken and the apple-onion mixture to the Dutch oven; heat to boiling. Reduce heat to low. Cover and simmer 45 minutes or until the chicken is fork tender.
7. Stir in the sour cream or yogurt. Cook until heated but do not boil.
8. Saute the nuts in butter and add to the mixture. Sprinkle the mint leaves over the top.

Use the best curry powder you can get. Try an Indian store
if there is one near you, or see what is available in the foreign
food section of the supermarket.

If you want the absolute best, you can make it yourself,
but omit ginger and curry from recipe on page 60.

CURRY POWDER

> 1 t ground coriander
> 1/2 t cayenne pepper
> 1/2 t ground cinnamon
> 1/2 t ground cloves
> 1/2 t ground ginger
> 1/2 t turmeric
> a pinch of ground cardamom
> 2 cloves garlic, crushed

Serves 6—8

Chicken & Cornmeal Italienne

This is a zesty meal that will stick to the ribs. Cornmeal polenta is a moist, crustless, bread-like substance made by stirring cornmeal into boiling water. Moog developed a taste for polenta during a business trip to Italy, where it is served with a delicate tomato sauce. I make it often in the winter, accompanied by a big tossed salad. Even my children love this dish.

    2 T olive oil
    2 T butter
    2 T coarsely chopped onion
    1 chicken (about 3 lb) cut into serving pieces
    1—2 cups chicken broth
    1 t salt
    pepper to taste
    1/4 t powdered thyme
    1/8 t dried sage
    1 T chopped parsley
    1 t sweet basil
    2 T chopped celery leaves
    a pinch of allspice and ground cloves
    1/2 cup white wine
    2 T tomato paste

1. Heat the oil and butter in a heavy skillet. Fry the onions golden. Remove and save.
2. Fry the chicken pieces in oil until brown. Sprinkle all the spices into the frying pan while the chicken is browning.
3. In a separate pan, simmer the onions in the chicken broth, and add the tomato paste.
4. Add the wine to the chicken and let it boil until it almost disappears.
5. Add the onion, broth and tomato paste mixture to the chicken. Cover loosely and simmer gently for about 30 minutes, or until the chicken is tender and the sauce has thickened a bit.
6. Serve over cornmeal.

Serves 6

CORNMEAL POLENTA

4 cups water
1 1/2 t salt
1 1/2 cups cornmeal *

1. Boil 3 cups of salted water in a deep, heavy pan.
2. Stir the remaining cup of water into the cornmeal. Pour this mixture into the boiling water, stirring constantly.
3. Lower the heat and simmer the polenta for about 45 minutes. Stir occasionally to prevent it from sticking to the bottom of the pan.

When the polenta is done, it will be very thick and have a lovely smell, like freshly baked bread.

Use a wooden spoon to arrange the polenta on a large platter. Serve the pieces of chicken over the polenta and cover with a layer of the lush sauce.

*If you can obtain it, use a course ground cornmeal. It has much more character.

Serves 4

Roasted Game Hens With Cheese & Sausage Stuffing

The electronic composer, John Eaton, is a red haired, plump cherub of a man who loves food—he waxes ecstatic over a dish he likes. When he was served roasted game hen, he called it "the left breast of Aphrodite."

I also served this dish on another occasion to Walter Carlos and Keith Emerson. They are both slim people and very particular eaters. They both loved it and expressed surprise that they were able to finish it.

> 2 rock cornish game hens
> 1 cup grated parmesan cheese
> 1 egg
> 1 finely chopped sprig of parsley
> 1 minced garlic clove
> 1/2 lb ground veal or pork, fried
> 1/2 t salt
> 1/4 t ground pepper

1. Combine all ingredients except the hens and mix thoroughly.
2. Stuff the hens with the mixture and secure the openings with poultry pins.
3. Rub the hens with bacon fat.
4. Roast at 325 degrees for 1 hour for a 1 lb. bird. For a 1 1/2 lb. bird, 1 hour and 15 minutes will be necessary. Baste the hens with the pan juices frequently.

To serve, cut the hens in half and arrange attractively on a platter. If you want a delicate gravy, thicken the pan juices with a little flour. A cooked green vegetable, salad and white wine are naturals for this meal.

A whole roasting chicken may take the place of the hens, but the presentation is not quite so festive. If you do substitute the roasting chicken, you will have to cook the bird longer than the time specified above.

Serves 4

Giblet Gravy For Poultry

1. Measure poultry giblets. Put them in a pot. Add twice as much water as the measured giblets. (1 cup giblets = 2 cups water.) Add bits of onion, carrots, celery, spinach, etc. to flavor broth. Cook over medium heat until giblets are tender.
2. When you are ready to make the gravy, add gizzard meat but discard gristle.
3. Put giblets (liver, heart, neck meat and gizzard meat) into the blender with enough stock to fill blender 3/4 full. Leave the soup greens and vegetables in the broth—they will add to the taste. Add 2–3 tablespoons flour to the mixture in the blender and blend until mixture is liquefied.
4. Pour resulting gravy base into pan. Simmer over low heat.
To chicken gravy, add salt, pepper and/or soy sauce.
To turkey gravy, also add Marmite, thyme, sage, or cumin.
The gravy may be stirred occasionally while it thickens over low heat. Take it off the stove when it reaches the consistency you want.

Tangy Creamed Turkey

This hearty dish is a great way to use leftover turkey. The sauce is creamy and tangy because of the yogurt and cumin.

        2 T butter
        1/4 lb mushrooms, sliced
        1/2 cup chopped onion
        1/4 cup chopped green pepper
        1 cup mayonnaise
        1 cup yogurt
        1/2 t salt
        a dash of pepper
        a pinch of cumin
        1 1/2 cups chopped cooked turkey
        1 cup cooked green peas

1. Melt butter in a skillet and add the mushrooms, onions and green peppers. Saute until tender.
2. Mix together the next 5 ingredients, and add to the sauteed vegetables.
3. Stir in the turkey and peas; cook over low heat until the mixture is warmed through. Serve the turkey over brown rice.

Serves 4

Hot Turkey Salad

When turkey legs are on sale, I like to buy them in quantity and freeze them for future use. Two large turkey legs are sufficient for this recipe.

I cook the legs slowly in a large pot for 3 or 4 hours with water and leftover vegetables. The meat can then be used in recipes calling for cooked turkey, and the broth makes an excellent soup base. If you have no immediate use for the broth, freeze it in ice cube trays for later use.

> 3 cups cooked diced turkey
> 2 cups celery, thinly sliced, including the
>   chopped celery leaves
> 1 cup sauteed bread cubes
> 1/2 cup sauteed almonds or unsalted cashews
> 1/2 t salt
> 2 t finely chopped onion
> 1 cup mayonnaise
> 2 T lemon juice
> 1/2 cup grated Cheddar or Parmesan cheese
> 1 or 2 chopped apples
> a pinch of curry powder and cumin

1. Mix all of the ingredients together except for the grated cheese.
2. Spread the mixture in a 9" X 12" casserole. Sprinkle the cheese over the top.
3. Bake at 350° for 20 minutes, or until hot and bubbly.

Stir-fry vegetables or a crisp salad go well with this dish.

Serves 4

Turkey Soup

This can be made with a turkey carcass or with turkey legs. It is such a hearty, thick, soup that you do not have to add the meat after the soup is made. Serve this with a good wheat bread and garbanzo spread.

    turkey carcass or legs
    2 onions, chopped
    3 minced cloves garlic
    1 cup celery pieces and chopped celery leaves
    4 T olive oil
    bay leaf
    1 t soy sauce or Marmite
    1 t cumin, ground
    1/2 cup bean sprouts
    1/4 t curry
    3 qts water
    1/4–1/2 cup barley
    4 large carrots, sliced or cubed
    1/4–1/2 cup tomatoes, puree or tomato ketchup
    1/2 lb fresh or frozen string beans
    2 cups spinach leaves in small pieces

1. Saute chopped onions, garlic, celery pieces and leaves in olive oil in soup kettle.
2. Add water, salt to taste, turkey, and tomato and cook until turkey is tender—2 hours if legs are used.
3. After you add the water and turkey, add bay leaf, soy sauce (or Marmite). cumin and curry.
4. When turkey is just about tender, add barley and carrot and cook 1/2 hour more on low heat.
5. Add string beans and cook for 15 minutes.
6. Remove turkey carcass or legs. Cool and strip all meat. Cut into small pieces and return to soup or use in turkey salad. Just before serving, add spinach leaves and bean sprouts.

Serves 7

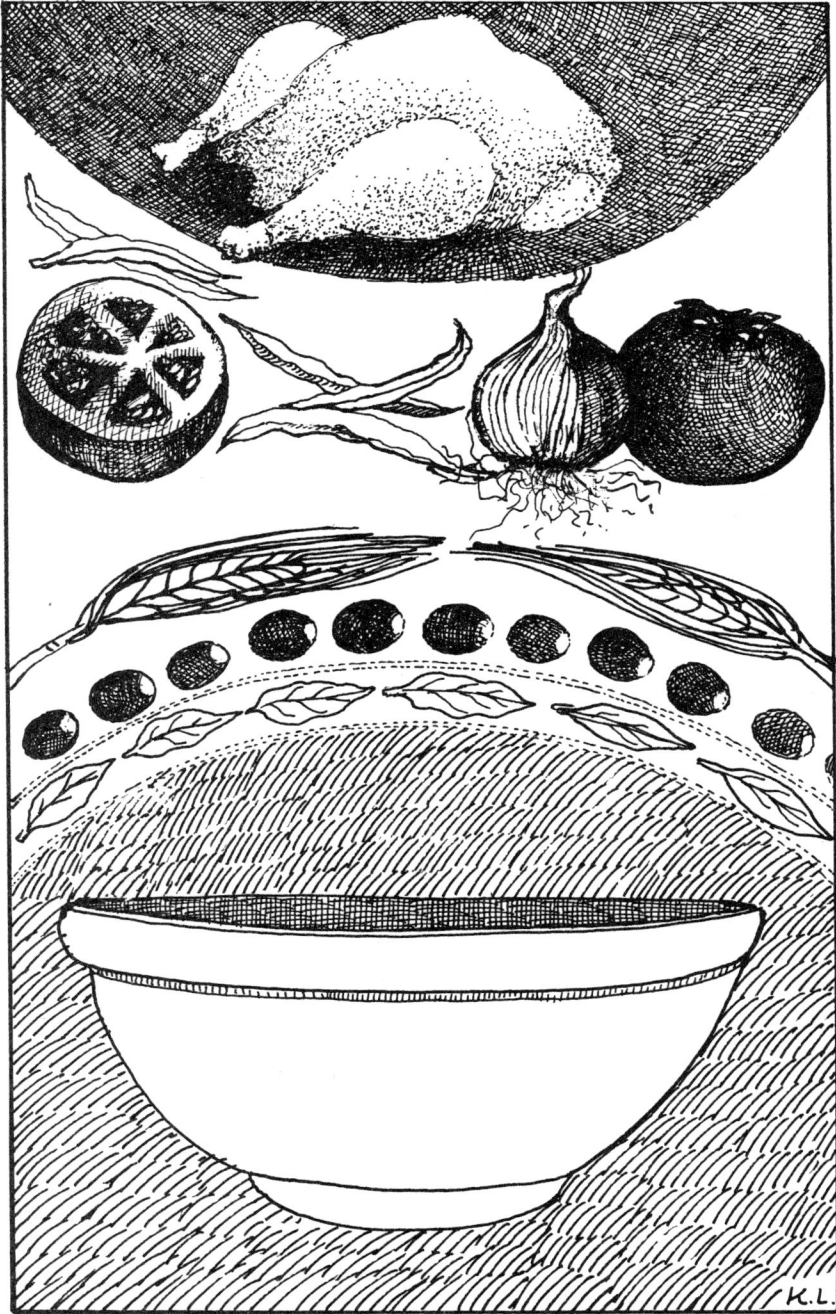

Ground Meat
Lamb & Wheat Meatballs (Kufte)

Moog doesn't always give me a lot of notice when he brings someone home for dinner. The night he brought Gerry MacDonald, a
musician—engineer, I was glad that I was serving Kufte, since a
little goes a long way. Gerry enjoyed the meal.

The lamb and wheat meatballs are stuffed with a spicy onion,
raisin and nut mixture.

> 1 cup cracked wheat*
> 1 1/2 lbs ground lamb (beef may be used)
> fresh ground pepper
> 1 small onion, chopped
> 2 T oil
> 2 T finely chopped almonds
> 2 T chopped parsley
> 2 T currants or raisins
> 1/4 t allspice
> 1 cup tomato juice
> 1 chicken bouillon cube
> 1/2 t each of thyme, sage and cumin
> 3 cups water

1. Blend together the wheat, meat, salt, pepper and herbs.
2. Saute the onion, parsley, currants, nuts and allspice in oil.
3. Form the meat mixture into approximately 18 balls. Make
a depression in the center of each and fill it with the onion-
parsley mixture. Smooth some of the meat mixture over the
depression so that the filling is sealed in.
4. Combine the tomato juice, bouillon cube and water in a
kettle and bring to a boil. Gently drop in the meatballs. Cover
and simmer for 25 minutes.
5. Remove the meatballs with a slotted spoon. Thicken the
gravy by adding a paste made of cornstarch and water (or whole
wheat flour and water), and boil for a few minutes. Return the
meatballs to the gravy and serve.

Salad and wine and some crusty bread complete the meal.

* Cracked wheat, also known as bulghur, is sold in bulk in Syrian or Lebanese stores and sometimes in natural food stores. Many supermarkets also carry it in boxes, but it is more expensive when you buy it this way.

Serves 4–6

Swedish Meatballs

Swedish meatballs are great as a main course or as an appetizer. Let the kids help—it speeds the project.

> **2 lbs meat loaf mixture (pork, veal and beef)**
> **2 eggs**
> **1/2 cup bread crumbs**
> **1/4 cup onions**
> **scant cup of milk**
> **2 t salt**
> **1/2 t nutmeg**
> **ground pepper, to taste**
> **1 cup beef bouillon**

1. Mix together all the ingredients except the beef bouillon. Roll the mixture into small meatballs about the diameter of a quarter.
2. Brown the meatballs under the broiler for about 10 minutes. Be sure to use a slotted broiler pan so that the fats will drain off properly.
3. Heat beef bouillon in a saucepan and simmer the browned meatballs in it for 20 minutes.
4. Remove the meatballs to a separate dish and thicken the bouillon sauce with 1 tablespoon cornstarch mixed with 1/4 cup water. Bring to a boil, stirring constantly. Boil until the sauce has the desired consistency, or is thick enough to coat a spoon. When the sauce has thickened, put the meatballs back in and warm through.

This dish can be served over spaetzle or brown rice.

Serves 6 for dinner or 8–10 for appetizers

Italian Meatballs

These meatballs plus a good tomato sauce are good over spaghetti or cornmeal polenta. If you want to use them for an appetizer or a buffet dish, shape them the size of ping-pong balls.

2 T olive oil
1/2 t oregano
1/4 t pepper
2 onions, chopped
1 T parsley, minced
3 cloves of garlic, minced
1/2 lb mushrooms
2 lbs meat loaf mix
1 cup chopped mozzarella or Swiss cheese
1/2 cup grated Parmesan cheese
1 cup bread crumbs
1 egg, slightly beaten
1 t salt
1 cup beef bouillon

1. Saute together the first seven ingredients until the onions become limp.
2. Mix the sauteed ingredients with all other ingredients except the beef bouillon. Form into large, egg size balls.
3. Simmer the meatballs in the beef bouillon about 1/2 hour or until done. Turn the meatballs once gently while simmering.

Serves 6—8

Cumin Meatballs

These meatballs are pungent and delicious.

> 2 lbs chopped chuck
> 1 egg
> 2 T parsley, minced
> 2 small onions, chopped fine
> 1 clove garlic, minced
> 1 cup bread crumbs
> salt and pepper to taste
> 1 1/2 t powdered cumin
> 1 1/2 t cumin seeds
> 1 1/2 cups beef bouillon

1. Saute together the onion and garlic.
2. Mix together all the ingredients except the bouillon. Shape into large, egg size meatballs. If necessary, add a tablespoon or two of the bouillon and the mixture will blend and shape easier.
3. Put the meatballs in a Dutch oven and pour the beef bouillon over them. Simmer slowly for approximately one hour and turn them once during the cooking time. Add more broth if needed.

Serve with kasha varnishkes, green salad and wine.

Serves 6—8

Sausage Stuffed Mushrooms

Mushrooms contain many nutrients on their outer skins. These nutrients can be washed off very easily, so please don't clean mushrooms by holding them under running water. Instead, wipe them gently with a damp cloth.

    16 large mushrooms
    6 oz sweet Italian sausage, uncased
    1 clove garlic, minced
    3 T olive oil
    2 T minced parsley
    1/4 cup grated Parmesan cheese

1. Clean the mushrooms. Remove the stems and chop them finely. Reserve the caps.
2. Heat 1 tablespoon of olive oil in a skillet and put in the uncased sausage, garlic and chopped mushroom stems. Break the sausage up with a fork and cook until lightly brown. Remove from heat.
3. Add 1 tablespoon oil, parsley and cheese to the sausage and mushroom mixture and blend together.
4. Fill the mushroom caps with the sausage mix.
5. Put the filled caps in a shallow pan one layer deep and add the remaining oil and 1/4 cup water to the pan. Bake in a pre-heated 350 degree oven for twenty minutes.

Serve these mushrooms with herb bread and tossed salad.

Serves 3 for dinner or 8 for appetizers

Stuffed Tufoli

This is a tasty, inexpensive meal. If you have children, have them scrub up and help you. They love stuffing the pipe shaped tufoli (pasta) with the chopped meat mix.

You can substitute a cheese mixture for the meat, if you wish, but the kids will not be able to handle it themselves. And the cheese filling is more expensive. The meat can be stretched, but the cheese cannot. See page 85 for the cheese filling.

I made the meat tufoli a great deal in our penny pinching days and still welcome the dish as a balance to some of our more costly meals.

> **1 lb tufoli, No. 43, or as large as you can get**
> **1/3 stick melted butter**
> **1 cup grated Parmesan cheese**
> **1 recipe Italian meatball mixture, page 72**
> **1/2 recipe tomato sauce, page 106**

1. Cook the tufoli in 6 quarts of rapidly boiling salted water until it is parboiled, about 12 minutes. Drain and rinse with cold water. Return to the pot and toss with the melted butter to prevent it from sticking together.
2. Make stuffing as specified for Italian meatballs.
3. Using a teaspoon or your hands, stuff the tufoli with the meat mixture.
4. Spread a thin layer of tomato sauce in a baking dish and arrange the stuffed tufoli, one layer only, over the sauce. Cover with the rest of the tomato sauce and sprinkle the Parmesan cheese over all.
5. Bake for 30 minutes in a 350°oven.

This recipe will fill a 10" x 12" pan and a 8" x 8" pan.

Serves 12

Apple Sausage Popover

2 large eggs
1 cup milk
1/4 t salt
1 T melted butter (unsalted)
1 cup flour
additional butter
1 t grated lemon rind
2 cups applesauce (homemade chunky is best)
2 T brown sugar
1/4 t cinnamon
1 t nutmeg
a dash of cloves
1 lb little sausages, cooked and drained

1. Preheat oven to 400°. Put 2 or 3 tablespoons of butter in a 10 inch cast iron skillet (or pyrex deep pie pan) and place it in the oven to heat.
2. Beat eggs till light and fluffy. Beat in milk, salt and melted butter. Stir in flour, 2 or 3 tablespoons at a time. Beat until batter is smooth and creamy.
3. Brush butter all over inside of preheated skillet and pour in the batter. Bake 30 minutes. Reduce heat to moderate and cook 10 minutes more. The popover should rise very high at the sides and dip in the middle to form a shell. If it doesn't cooperate, prick the center with a fork to form a depression.
4. While popover bakes, mix apple sauce, sugar and spices in a saucepan and cook 3 or 4 minutes. Stir in lemon rind.
5. Cook and drain sausages according to this method which I think is the best. Place sausages in skillet with half cup water and cover. Bring to a boil and allow to simmer for 8 minutes. Then drain off water and brown sausages over low heat, uncovered. This results in golden brown, juicy sausages, rather than dried up, chewy ones.
6. To serve, spread hot apple sauce in popover shell; top with hot sausages arranged in a pinwheel. Cut in generous wedges.

Serves 6

Meat Pie Yannina

This recipe makes a huge amount. When accompanied by a salad, it easily serves my family of 6 for two meals. It also makes good hors d'oeuvres when cut into smaller pieces.

The recipe can be reduced by half, if that is more practical for you.

> 2 lbs chopped lamb, or meat loaf mix
> 8 eggs, slightly beaten, and 1 egg yolk
> 3 cups milk
> 2 cups dry bread crumbs
> 1 cup grated Parmesan cheese
> 1/2 cup chopped onions
> 4 T butter
> 3 T tomato paste
> 6 T chopped parsley
> salt and pepper to taste
> 2 T ground cumin
> 1/4 t cinnamon
> double pie crust for a 10" x 16" pan*

1. Brown the onion in butter.
2. Add the chopped meat and brown slightly.
3. Add tomato paste diluted in a glass of water, salt and pepper, and simmer until the water is evaporated. Remove from the heat.
4. Add the milk, eggs, cheese, bread crumbs, parsley, salt and pepper, cumin and cimmamon.
5. Line the baking dish with half of the pie crust. Then add the meat filling. Cover with the other half of the pie crust, trim and make slits in the top to allow the steam to escape while baking. Brush the top crust with egg yolk.
6. Bake in a preheated 350° oven for 45 to 50 minutes.

Serve hot with a Greek salad containing feta cheese.

* Use the pie crust recipe on page 89.

Serves 12

Stuffed Cabbage Rolls

This is one of Moog's favorites. It is a true one pot meal because it contains a vegetable, meat and starch all in one dish.

1 large head of cabbage
1 lb meat loaf mix
1/2 cup raw brown rice
1 chopped onion
2 minced cloves garlic
1/4 cup butter
1 egg
2 t salt
a dash of ground pepper
1/2 t thyme
1 t dill
2 t parsley
1 lb sauerkraut, drained
1 can (28 oz) tomato sauce, plain

1. Cut the center core out of the head of cabbage.
2. Put the cabbage in a kettle with 4 to 6 inches of water and bring to a boil. Remove the leaves of the cabbage as they cook and wilt. The leaves do not have to be cooked completely; they just need to be soft and flexible. Use tongs to prevent scalding your fingers. Save 1 1/2 cups of the cabbage water.
3. Cut a V from the base of each leaf to eliminate the coarse central rib.
4. Brown the onion and garlic in butter.
5. Mix the ground meat with rice, chopped onion, garlic, egg, salt and pepper and the other herbs.
6. Put a large spoonful of the meat mixture in the center of the 20 largest cabbage leaves. Fold the edges of the leaves over the meat and then roll tightly.
7. Chop up the remaining cabbage leaves. Layer the bottom of a kettle with half of the chopped leaves and place the cabbage rolls over them. Top with the remaining chopped cabbage leaves, sauerkraut, tomato sauce, butter and 1 1/2 cups of boiling water, saved from the kettle the cabbage was boiled in.

Cover and simmer for about an hour, or until the cabbage rolls are tender.

Whole grain bread and beer or wine will make this a very satisfying meal. If you wish to take advantage of the lush juice, serve the rolls on a bed of brown rice or cornmeal or just get in there with your bread and sop it up.

Serves 4—6

Beef & Veal
Herbed Goulash

This herbed goulash served over dilled spaetzle is a truly synergistic combination.

        2 1/2 lbs chuck steak, or a roast, cut into
                1 1/2"cubes
        2 T beef drippings or shortening
        3 cups coarsely chopped onion
        1 clove garlic, minced
        1 can (8 oz) tomato sauce
        2 T brown sugar
        1 T Hungarian paprika
        1 1/2 t salt
        1 t caraway seed
        1 t dill seed
        1 t Worcestershire sauce
        1/4 t pepper
        1/2 pint sour cream or yogurt (optional)

1. Brown the meat on all sides in the drippings or shortening.
2. Add onion, garlic, tomato sauce and seasonings. Mix carefully.
3. Cover and cook slowly until beef cubes are tender. This should take about 1 1/2 or 2 hours.
4. If desired, stir in the yogurt or sour cream just before serving.

Serves 6

Oriental Beef & Carrots

This is a cinch to make. The marinating time is 4–8 hours. After that, the dish takes no time at all.

> 2 lbs flank steak
> soy sauce
> 3 cloves minced garlic
> 6 minced scallions
> 2 T sugar
> peanut or olive oil
> 2 or 3 carrots, peeled and sliced on the
>   diagonal
> 1 medium onion, chopped fine

1. Slice the flank steak in thin slices across the grain and put in a bowl.
2. Add all the other ingredients. Use enough oil and soy sauce to coat the meat and vegetables generously. You should use a little more oil than soy sauce. Marinate 8 hours, turning 3 or 4 times. While it is marinating, it should be covered tightly and kept in a cool place. If you are short of time, the meat can be marinated for only 3 or 4 hours, but the longer marinating time will greatly improve the flavor.

3. Use a large baking dish or line a broiling pan with foil and arrange the meat slices and carrots on it. Include as much of the sauce as you can without overflowing. Broil until the meat is cooked and the carrots are warmed but still crunchy, about 15–20 minutes.
4. Serve the meat over brown rice with the carrots on top.

Serves 6

Marinated Skirt Steak Roulades

Skirt steak is a long, thin steak that comes one per cow. My butcher saves them for me. Perhaps yours will too, if you ask him. It is tasty and juicy. It is slightly expensive, but there is absolutely no waste. It may be broiled, but marinating the beef produces more tender results.

> 2 1/2 lbs skirt steak
> 1/2 cup olive oil
> 3/4 cup red wine
> 1/4 cup soy sauce
> 2 small onions, chopped
> 1—2 t ground pepper
> 1 T minced parsley

1. Skirt steak comes in a long rectangle (see diagram) which you can cut in half the short way. Then cut the sections into pieces 1/4 to 1/2" wide, going the long way. Roll the sections like a pinwheel or Danish pastry, using the smaller pieces inside the pinwheel, with the longer pieces outside. Secure with round toothpicks—the flat ones break easily.
2. Mix the ingredients for the marinade. Put the meat into the marinade and let it stand 2—3 hours. Turn it once.
3. Broil 10—15 minutes until crispy looking but not dried out. Watch carefully. Marinated meats cook much faster than non marinated meats.
4. Serve with sauteed mushrooms or onions, accompanied by kasha or brown rice and salad.

Serves 6

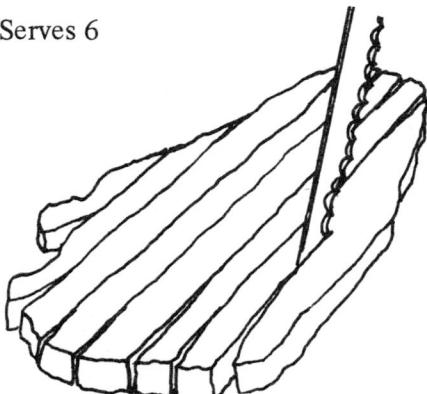
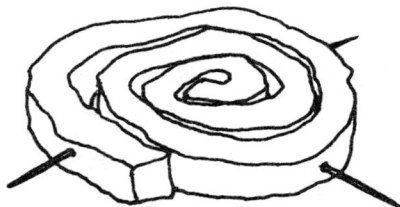

Veal Milanese

This dish is so simple, it's almost not a recipe, but the results are ultra civilized

> 2 lbs veal cutlets
> olive oil
> 2 cloves garlic, slivered
> 1 t oregano
> bread crumbs
> beaten egg
> 1 lemon, cut into quarters

1. Pound the cutlets with a wooden mallet until thin, and then cut them into pieces about the size of a fifty cent piece.
2. Dip the meat pieces in egg and bread crumbs and fry in hot olive oil with the garlic slivers and oregano, until the meat is golden brown.
3. Garnish with the lemon wedges.

Broccoli in cheese sauce, spinach salad and a white wine complete the meal very nicely.

Serves 8

Veal Dagmar

Ray Dolby is a pioneer in the field of noise reduction. Ray's name can be seen on the back of record jackets, tape decks, cassettes, etc. While Moog and I were in London in 1969, the Dolbys were our hosts. Dagmar made this dish for us—I adopted it as soon as I returned home.

This recipe, like the preceding one, is extremely simple to prepare. It is also very flexible and can accommodate as many guests as you please. Just plan on a half lb. of veal per person and adjust the other ingredients.

> **2 lbs veal cutlets**
> **flour**
> **butter**
> **salt**
> **pepper**
> **1/2 lb tiny peas, fresh or frozen***
> **1/2 lb mushrooms, cleaned and sliced**
> **1 cup sour cream**

1. Pound the veal until it is thin, and cut into pieces about the size of a fifty cent piece.
2. Coat the meat with flour and then fry in hot butter until golden.
3. Cook the peas and drain them.
4. Saute the mushrooms in butter in a large pan.
5. Add the fried cutlets and cooked peas to the mushrooms. Season to taste with salt and pepper.
6. Add sour cream to make a consistency that pleases you. Stir until warm, but don't let the sour cream get too hot or it may curdle.

Serve over rice or spaetzle.

*Buy Green Giant LeSeur tiny peas in butter sauce at your supermarket freezer section. They are the sweetest small peas except for garden fresh peas.

Serves 4—6

Cheese & Eggs
Manicotti In Crepe Covers

This dish is much more delicate than pasta manicotti. The simple crepe covers transform a hearty peasant dish to a delicate gourmet treat. Excellent with salad and garlic bread.

> 1 1/2 lbs ricotta cheese
> salt and pepper to taste
> 1 egg
> 1/2 cup diced ham (optional)
> 3 T minced parsley
> 1 cup grated Parmesan cheese
> 18–24 crepe covers, see page 86
> about 2 cups tomato sauce, see page 106

1. Mix together the first 5 ingredients.
2. Place one tablespoon of the cheese mixture on each cooked crepe, and fold the crepes into rectangles.
3. Spread a thin layer of tomato sauce in a 10" x 12" baking dish and place the crepes on it, seam side down.
4. Cover the crepes with a modest amount of tomato sauce, and sprinkle the grated Parmesan cheese over all. Bake in a 350° oven until the sauce is bubbly, about 15 minutes.

Makes 18–24 manicotti

1. spoon on filling

3. tuck in ends

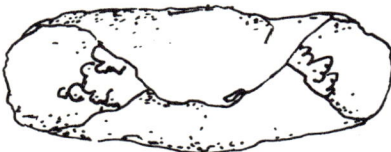

2. fold over filling

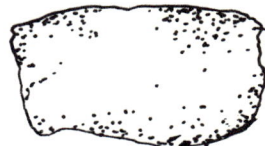

4. place seam side down in pan

Mom's Blintzes

Joel Chadabe teaches music at the State University of New York, Albany. When he tasted my blintzes, he exclaimed, "I'll never buy Milady's again!"

Crepe Covers

> 1 cup flour
> 2 cups cold water
> 12 beaten eggs
> 1/2 t salt
> 18–24 t butter or margarine

Cheese Filling

> 2 lbs pot cheese*
> 1 lb farmers cheese*
> 4 eggs
> 2–4 T sugar
> 1 t vanilla
> 1/4 cup raisins, optional
> 1/4 cup chopped or ground nuts

1. Combine the first 4 ingredients in a large bowl and beat together.
2. Melt a teaspoon of the butter or margarine in a small fry pan. It should be as hot as you can get it without burning. (Margarine will not burn as easily as butter.) Tip the pan so that oil covers half way up the sides as well as the bottom of the pan
3. Pour about 1/4 cup of the batter into pan and quickly swirl it around the bottom and half way up the sides of the pan. Fry till the bottom of the crepe is golden brown and no longer sticks to the pan. Run a spatula around the sides of the crepe to make sure it is loose. Turn the crepe out onto a platter, browned side up.

Repeat steps 2 and 3 for each individual crepe. If you've never made crepes before, you may want to regard the first two or three crepes as test runs, until you get a feel for it.

4. While the finished crepes are cooling, combine the last 7 ingredients to make the cheese filling.

5. Put a heaping tablespoon of the cheese filling into the center of each cold crepe, and then fold them into squares.

6. Place them folded side down in a greased 9" x 13" pan, and put a dot of butter on top of each blintz.

7. Bake at 325° for 30 to 45 minutes, until the tops turn brown and puff up. You can run them under the broiler *briefly,* if you want them browner.

Serve two or three blintzes per person, with a dollop of sour cream and homemade strawberry preserves on top. They are lovely with a cold white or rose wine. They are also a really boss breakfast treat!

*If you can't obtain pot and farmer cheese, substitute partially creamed cottage cheese and cream cheese. If you use creamed cottage cheese, strain it so that most of the liquid drains out first. You should also add about 1/2 cup of ground nuts to prevent the filling from being runny.

Fresh or dried herbs can be substituted for the fruit and nuts. Try parsley, dill and celery leaves. If you use herbs, omit the jam and serve with a big, tossed salad.

If you have any blintzes left over, they freeze beautifully.

Makes 18—24 blintzes

Onion Quiche

I started making quiche when we had very little money and eggs were cheap. All that's needed to turn out a classy meal is a bit of finesse. A spinach salad and good bread go well with quiche.

  6 slices bacon
  3 onions, sliced thin
  4 eggs
  1 tall can evaporated milk (1 2/3 cups)
          or heavy cream
  2/3 cup water
  3/4 t salt
  1 t dry mustard
  a dash of Tabasco sauce
  1/2 t Hungarian paprika
  1 t soy sauce
  1 cup grated Cheddar cheese
  1 clove garlic, minced
  1 9" pie shell (see following recipe)

1. Cook the bacon and, when there is plenty of bacon fat in the pan, add the onion and garlic. Cook until the bacon is done and the onions are golden. Crumble the bacon.
2. Combine the eggs, evaporated milk, water, salt, dry mustard, soy sauce, Tabasco and paprika. Beat with a rotary beater just long enough to mix thoroughly.
3. Sprinkle the pie shell with the crumbled bacon, the onion, garlic, Cheddar cheese and any remaining bacon grease. Sauteed mushrooms and bits of ham may also be added. Pour the egg and milk mixture in also.
4. Bake in a preheated oven at 325° for one hour, or until the point of a knife inserted in the center of the quiche comes out clean.

PIE SHELL

This recipe makes enough dough for two pie shells. If you need only one shell, freeze the second shell or divide the recipe in half.

- **1 cup white flour**
- **1 cup whole wheat flour (pastry if possible)**
- **1 t baking powder**
- **1/2 t salt**
- **1/2 cup shortening or lard***
- **4–6 T ice water**

1. Mix the dry ingredients together.
2. Cut the lard into the dry ingredients until it is in small pieces.
3. Mix in enough ice water so that the dough will hold together. Mix the dough gently with your hands, and form into a big ball.
4. Divide the dough in half. Roll half the dough on a floured board with a floured rolling pin, turning the dough in a circle movement to get a nice round shape.
5. To move the dough from the board to the pie plate, fold it into quarters and then gently unfold it when it is centered in the plate. Shape the crust into the plate and trim the edges.

*When you use this recipe for Quiche or Meat Pie, use bacon fat. When you use this recipe for Apple Pie, use shortening or lard and add grated cheese.

Serves 6

Omelettes

The kind of omelette I like to make takes a bit of describing. I use a rectangular, teflon coated griddle that straddles two burners. If the omelette is for breakfast, I grease the griddle with butter; if it is for lunch or dinner, I grease it with olive oil and season it with garlic and oregano.

When the grease is hot, I pour on enough beaten eggs to cover the griddle completely and then distribute the filling in three intervals over the omelette. When the eggs have set, I use two pancake flippers to roll up the omelette from short end to short end. I then pivot it around on the griddle and cook it until the omelette is golden brown and the filling is hot.

This produces a delicate, well filled omelette. I much prefer it to the thicker variety made in a divided omelette pan.

Six eggs will make an omelette for three people, eight eggs for four people.

A light tomato sauce can be poured over the folded omelette when it is served. A salad, muffins and wine complete the menu for a simple but tasty meal.

Suggested Fillings

> sauteed onions
> sauteed onions with mushrooms and/or cheese
> sliced or grated cheese
> cheese and bits of ham or sausage

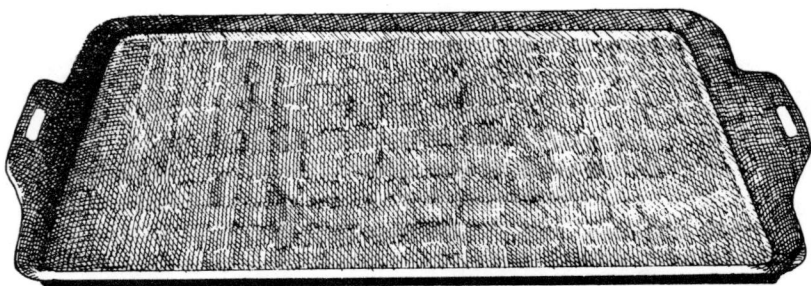

Cottage Cheese Pancakes

These pancakes are very light. They are delicious served with honey or maple syrup with applesauce or rhubarb. I never have leftovers. Serve for breakfast or a light supper.

> **3 eggs, separated**
> **1/4 t salt**
> **1/2 cup flour plus 2 or 3 T (use half white,**
> **half whole-wheat)**
> **3/4 cup cottage cheese**

1. Beat the egg whites until they are stiff but not dry.
2. Beat the egg yolks until they are a light lemon color. Stir the salt, flour and cottage cheese into the beaten yolks.
3. Fold the egg whites in.
4. Drop the batter by the tablespoon on a hot, heavily greased griddle. I use margarine rather than butter to keep the pancakes from sticking. I also keep the margarine very hot before I drop the pancakes on the griddle.) Before you turn the pancakes, be sure to check to see the bottoms are nicely browned.

This recipe makes 16 small pancakes or enough for 2 or 3 people. I double or triple the recipe to feed my family of 6.

Eggplant Manicotti

This dish has much to recommend it. It is tasty, inexpensive, quick to make, low in calories, and meatless. What more could you ask?

> 2 medium size eggplants
> 2 eggs
> 1/2 cup flour
> 1/2 cup water
> 3 or 4 T olive oil
> a pinch of basil and oregano
> 1 clove garlic, minced
> 1 lb ricotta or cottage cheese
> 1/4 lb mozzarella or Swiss sheese, diced
> 1/2 cup Parmesan cheese, grated
> 2 T finely chopped parsley
> 2 cups spaghetti sauce

1. Peel the eggplants and cut into lengthwise slices about 1/2" thick.
2. Make a batter by mixing together the flour and water with one egg.
3. Dip the eggplant slices in the batter and fry them in olive oil, basil, garlic and oregano. Cook until golden on each side and drain on paper towels.
4. Mix together the second egg, ricotta or cottage cheese, mozzarella or Swiss cheese, Parmesan cheese, parsley, salt and pepper. I prefer to use cottage cheese in this recipe because it makes the manicotti firmer.
5. Spread one cup of spaghetti sauce over the bottom of a 10" x 12" baking dish.
6. Spoon about 1/3 cup of the cheese mixture into the center of each eggplant slice and roll up the slices, starting at the narrow end.
7. Arrange the rolled eggplant slices in a single layer in the baking pan, seam side down. Sprinkle with Parmesan.

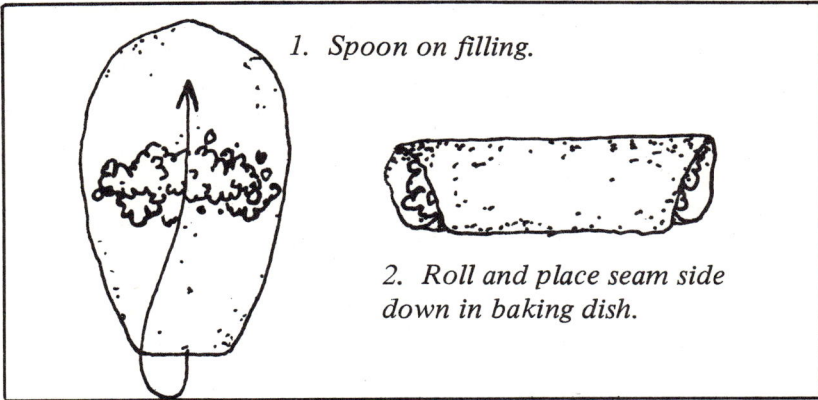

1. *Spoon on filling.*

2. *Roll and place seam side down in baking dish.*

8. Pour the remaining sauce over the manicotti and sprinkle with the Parmesan cheese.

9. Bake in a 350° oven for 25 minutes, or until bubbly hot.

Serves 6—8

Cheese Sandwiches

People who have to eat in restaurants a lot usually love home-made food, even if it's very simple. Not only is the food generally of better quality—the atmosphere is generally much more relaxed.

Cheese and eggs have been my standbys for a long time. If you always have on hand one good all purpose cheese, eggs, good bread and muffins, you'll be ready to entertain.

**homemade bread or any good store bread
any type of cheese**

Simply layer the sliced cheese over pieces of bread and broil until the cheese is melted. Serve warm.

These sandwiches can be served at breakfast with fresh juice or with fruit and coffee or tea. For a casual lunch or supper, serve them with Dijon mustard, pickles, wine or beer, fresh fruit and a sweet dessert.

Greek Spinach Pie

This is a delicate cheese and vegetable pie with a flaky, buttered crust. Swiss chard can be substituted for the spinach.

    1/4 cup olive oil
    1/2 cup minced onions
    1/4 cup minced scallions
    2 lbs fresh spinach, washed, drained and minced.
            or 2 boxes of frozen, chopped spinach,
            well drained.
    2 T dried dill weed
    1/4 cup minced parsley
    1/2 t salt
    ground pepper to taste
    1/3 cup milk
    1/2 lb feta cheese, finely crumbled
    4 eggs, lightly beaten
    1/2 lb butter, melted
    16 sheets (1/2 lb) filo pastry, each about
            12" x 16"

1. In a heavy skillet heat the olive oil over medium heat. Add the onions and scallions and cook for 5 minutes, stirring frequently.
2. Stir in the spinach and cover. Cook for 5 more minutes.
3. Add the dill, parsley, salt and pepper. Stir constantly for about 10 minutes over the heat, or until most of the liquid has evaporated.
4. Transfer the spinach mixture to a deep bowl and stir in the milk.
5. Cool to room temperature and add the cheese. Beat in the eggs slowly.
6. Preheat the oven to 300°.
7. With a pastry brush, coat the bottom and sides of a 2" x 7" x 12" baking dish with melted butter. Line the dish with a sheet of filo folded in half to 8" x 12", firmly pressing the edges of the pastry into the corners and against

the sides of the dish. Brush the sheet with 2 or 3 teaspoons of the melted butter, being careful to spread the butter over the entire sheet. Repeat this process with 7 more filo sheets.

8. Spread the spinach mixture over the eighth filo sheet.

9. Place the other sheets over the spinach, buttering each sheet as you did for the bottom layer. Brush the top of the pie with the remaining butter.

10. Bake in the middle of the oven for 1 hour, until the pastry is crisp.

11. Cut into squares and serve hot with a dry white wine, or a Greek retsina wine.

Filo leaves can usually be purchased by the pound in Greek grocery stores. They are also very good for making strudel.

Serves 6—8

Gazpacho

This tomato based soup is served cold. It makes a delightful meal for a hot summer day, as Max Matthews of Bell Labs will remember.

2 cups canned tomatoes or skinned fresh
      tomatoes
1 onion, chopped
1 green pepper, chopped
1 cucumber, chopped
1/2 cup red wine
1 clove garlic
salt and pepper to taste

2 T fresh lemon juice
2 cups tomato or V-8 juice
1/2 cup olive oil
1/4 t ground cumin
1 T Hungarian paprika

1. Combine the first 7 ingredients in a blender and puree for 30 seconds. Pour into a large bowl.
2. Add the last 5 ingredients to the pureed mix. Stir and refrigerate for 2 hours or more to chill.
3. While the soup is chilling, make croutons by sauteeing 1 cup of rye bread cubes in 3 T butter with 1 minced clove of garlic. Fry till crisp and golden.
4. Serve the gazpacho with small bowls of croutons, chopped onion, chopped green pepper, chopped cucumber and sliced black olives.

Herb bread, butter, cold white wine, fruit and cheese complete the meal.

Serves 6–8

Spinach, Egg & Cheese Bake

When Moog was in graduate school at Cornell getting his degree, he had a wonderful advisor named Henri Sack. Dr. Sack and his wife Lotte had two yearly bashes for his advisees: one big picnic in the summer and a Christmas special. This dish always showed up at the Christmas dinner—it was loved by everyone.

> 1—1 1/2 lbs spinach (or 2 boxes frozen
>   spinach)
> 4 hard boiled eggs, quartered
> 1/4 lb sliced or grated cheese (You can
>   use Cheddar, Parmesan, Swiss
>   or mozzerella)
> 2 T butter
> 2 T flour
> 1 cup warm milk
> nutmeg
> salt and pepper

1. Cook the spinach, drain and chop it. (The liquid can be saved for soup stock.)
2. Make a white sauce by melting the butter. Add the flour and stir it in quickly. Mix in the milk with a whisk and season with nutmeg, salt and pepper.
3. Blend the white sauce with the chopped spinach. Gently mix in the quartered eggs. Put the mixture in an 8" x 8" baking pan. Top with the cheese.
4. Bake in a 350° oven 20—30 minutes, or until bubbly hot. If the cheese isn't brown enough, you can put it under the broiler for a minute.

Serves 4—6

Seafood
Crab Stuffed Mushrooms

These stuffed mushrooms are really special. Served with a hearty salad, garlic bread and wine, it makes an elegant meal. Served alone, they are superb appetizers.

> 1 lb mushrooms, large
> 1/4 lb sweet butter, melted
> 1 can (6 1/2 oz) snow crab, drained
> 2 eggs
> 2–3 T mayonnaise
> 1/4 cup finely chopped scallions
> 4 t lemon juice
> 1/2 t Worchestershire or soy sauce
> 1/2 cup bread crumbs, or matzo meal,
>   with a pinch of oregano
> salt and pepper

1. Peel the mushrooms by reaching under the cap and peeling off the outermost layer of skin. Trim the mushrooms and separate the caps from the stems.
2. Mix the crabmeat, eggs, mayonnaise, scallions, lemon juice, Worchestershire or soy sauce, half the crumbs, salt and pepper.
3. Dip the mushroom caps in melted butter and place top down in a buttered baking dish.
4. Stuff the caps with the crab mixture. Sprinkle the rest of the crumbs over them and pour the remainder of the melted butter on top.
5. Bake in a preheated 375° oven for 15–20 minutes

A less expensive, but equally delicate and tasty version of this dish may be made by sauteeing a couple of pieces of flounder or haddock and substituting it for the crab. Flake the fish before adding it to the other ingredients.

Serves 2–3 for dinner or 6–8 for appetizers

Crab Fu Yong

Light and tasty, these pancakes are delightful served with brown rice and stir-fry vegetables.

>1 cup snow crab meat
>1 cup bean sprouts
>1/2 cup finely sliced celery
>3 T peanut oil
>1/2 cup shredded onion
>6 eggs
>1 T soy sauce
>1 T cornstarch
>1/2 t salt
>dash of pepper

1. Mix together the crab meat and sprouts in a bowl.
2. Saute the celery and onion in oil for about 5 minutes and add to the crab meat.
3. Beat together the eggs, soy sauce, cornstarch, salt and pepper. Pour over the crabmeat mixture and mix thoroughly.
4. Drop the crab meat batter by tablespoons on a greased griddle or skillet and brown on both sides.
6. Keep the pancakes warm until all are cooked.
7. Make the sauce below, and pour it over the tops of the pancakes before serving.

SAUCE

>1/2 cup water or chicken broth
>1 T sherry or brandy
>1 T soy sauce
>2 t cornstarch

1. Combine all of the ingredients in a saucepan and cook until thick.

If you don't have crab meat or don't want to use it, you can substitute 2 cups of bean sprouts. Use fresh sprouts if you can get them. They have a more delicate texture and taste than canned ones.

Serves 4

100/Main Courses, Seafood

Tuna Souffle

This has a lovely celery taste. It is inexpensive and looks very elegant when brought to table, golden and fragrant.

> 3 T butter
> 2 or 3 T minced celery stalks and leaves
> 2 or 3 T all purpose flour
> 1 cup warm milk
> 1 can (about 6 1/2 oz) light or white tuna,
>   drained and flaked
> 1/2 t lemon juice
> 1/8 t pepper
> 5 eggs, separated

1. Butter a 1 1/2 quart souffle dish.
2. In a medium saucepan over low heat, melt the butter. Add the onion and celery until softened. Blend in flour.
3. Add the milk. Cook and stir with a wire whisk over low heat until thick, smooth and bubbly. Remove from heat.
4. Stir in flaked tuna, lemon juice and pepper.
5. Beat the egg yolks and stir into sauce.
6. With a clean beater, beat the egg whites until they hold stiff, straight peaks.
7. Add about a quarter of the beaten egg whites to the tuna and mix in thoroughly. Gently fold in the remaining whites.
8. Turn into the prepared souffle dish.
9. Bake at 375° until the souffle has risen above the rim of the dish and is lightly browned, about 35 minutes. This must be served immediately.

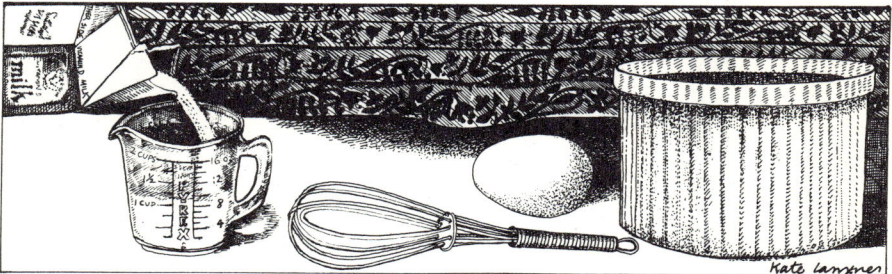

Fish Chowder

This chowder gets better as it ages, and the tastes mingle.

1/4 lb smoked bacon
3 large onions, sliced
4 medium potatoes
2 cups water
1 lb fillet of haddock
    or 2 cans minced clams
1/4 cup butter or bacon fat
1/4 cup flour
4 cups milk—skim is OK
1 1/2 t salt
1 t sugar
1/4 t pepper
pinch thyme & rosemary
1-14 oz can evaporated milk

1. Cut bacon into small pieces and cook until crisp. Add onions when fat begins to flow and saute until golden.
2. Peel and cube potatoes and add to onions. Cover with water and cook until potatoes are tender but not mushy.
3. Add small pieces of fish or clams and simmer for a few minutes.
4. Make a sauce with the butter flour, milk, salt, sugar and pepper. See page 97 for instructions but omit nutmeg. Use thyme and rosemary instead.
6. Add evaporated milk and simmer gently 10 minutes.
7. Serve hot. If you have any left over, be careful to warm it up slooowly in order to keep it in good shape.

Makes about 3 qts. Serves 10–12

Pasta

Spaghetti With White Clam Sauce

Herb Deutsch, of Hofstra University, and his family enjoyed this meal one evening.

1/2 lb spaghetti
2 cloves garlic, minced
1/2 t salt
1/2 t oregano
1/4 cup butter
2 T olive oil
1 6 oz can minced clams
1/4 cup Parmesan cheese
1/2 cup chopped parsley

1. Heat oil, butter, salt, garlic and oregano in fry pan.
2. When very hot, add drained clams and cook for a minute or two. Add 1/2 cup chopped parsley and toss well.
3. Pour over cooked and drained spaghetti and toss. Sprinkle with Parmesan cheese and freshly ground pepper.

4. Cook spaghetti according to directions. When done to your liking, drain in a colander and transfer to a large bowl. Put a plentiful dollop of butter on top, mix thoroughly. The butter will keep the pasta from sticking and make it easy to serve.

Fish fillets, (turbot, flounder, perch etc.) may be substituted. Flake with a fork before adding to the spaghetti.

Serves 2–3

Genovese Noodles Al Pesto

Genovese noodles, full of green herbs, oil and garlic, are a favorite of composer Joel Chadabe. He asked me how to make the sauce and was amused by my answer. "You put the oil, herbs and garlic in the blender, turn the dial and wop, there it is."

    1 lb noodles, spaghetti, or linguine
    1/2 cup butter, melted
    2 cups parsley leaves
    1 T basil
    1–1 1/2 t salt
    1/2 t ground pepper
    2 cloves garlic
    1/2 cup olive oil
    1/2 cup grated Parmesan cheese
    2 T pine nuts (pignoli), sesame seeds, or
        sunflower kernels (optional)

1. Cook and drain the noodles.
2. While the noodles are cooking, combine the butter, parsley, basil, salt, pepper, garlic, oil, cheese and nuts in the container of the electric blender. Whirl at high speed until smooth.
3. Pour over the noodles and toss lightly.

Clams or small pieces of fish may be lightly sauteed in olive oil and garlic and served over the noodles. Dried herbs may be used if you wish but the pungent aroma will be slightly diminished.

Serves 4–6

Fusilli With Cauliflower

See page 30 for details on this dish.

    1 lb fusilli (pasta in spirals)
    1 small cauliflower
    1 large onion, diced
    1 No. 2 can tomatoes
    4 T olive oil
    1 T pignoli (pine nuts)
    2 T currants
    3 anchovy filets, cut in small pieces
    salt and pepper to taste

1. Wash cauliflower. Break or cut cauliflower into small pieces.
2. Cook in rapidly boiling salted water until tender but not soft (10–12 minutes). Drain and set aside.
3. Heat oil in saucepan. Add onion and cook 3 minutes or until soft.
4. Add anchovies and stir a couple of minutes or until dissolved.
5. Add tomatoes, and simmer 20 minutes, covered.
6. Add pine nuts, currants, cauliflower and a pinch of salt and pepper. Mix well and keep hot over a low flame.
7. Cook fusilli in 4 quarts of rapidly boiling salted water 15 minutes or until tender.
8. Drain pasta and place in bowl. Add sauce. Serve very hot. Sprinkle with Romano cheese

Serves 4–6

Spaghetti With Tomato Sauce

I was never quite happy with my tomato sauce until I found this recipe. The addition of the cheese at the end gives the taste and texture I was looking for.

Tomato sauce is a great thing to keep on hand for super quick meals. Served over pasta (or polenta), it makes a complete main course.

> 1 large onion
> 2 cloves garlic, minced
> 1/4 cup olive oil
> 2 cans, 2 lb 3 oz each, Italian tomatoes
> packed in puree
> 2 cans, 6 oz each, tomato paste
> 2 T sugar or 1 grated carrot
> 1 T leaf oregano, crumbled
> 1 T basil
> 1–2 t salt
> 1 t ground pepper
> 1/2–1 cup grated Parmesan cheese

1. Saute the onion and garlic with the olive oil in a large soup pot.
2. Add the tomatoes, tomato paste, sugar (or carrot), oregano, basil, and salt and pepper and stir together. Simmer uncovered at least 45 minutes, but two or three hours would be better.
3. When the sauce is done, add the grated cheese and serve in a bowl. If the tomato sauce needs thinning, use red wine. It adds to the robust taste.
4. Accompany this with a bowl of cooked spaghetti liberally laced with melted butter and parsley.

This sauce freezes beautifully.

Makes enough sauce for spaghetti for 12

Side Dishes

Side Dishes

† **Easy recipes for the inexperienced hostess.**

‡ **These recipes can be frozen.**

Grains

Spaetzle

These are small, light, delicate, wave shaped Hungarian noodles made on the spot. They are pure, easy and fast. My children still think it's magic that one moment we have a bowl of batter and minutes later a big bowl of dilly buttered noodles.

> **dill weed**
> **1/4 t baking powder**
> **2 1/2 cups flour**
> **2 eggs**
> **1/2 cup milk**
> **1/2 cup water**

1. Mix together the wet ingredients. Mix slowly into dry ingredients. If the batter seems too heavy, add water.
2. Drop the batter into boiling salted water until the spaetzle come to the surface. (I use a spaetzle maker. It looks like a food mill, with bigger holes at the bottom. If you can't find one in a kitchen supply store, drop small bits of batter from a spoon.) Scoop up with a slotted spoon and drain. Continue until all batter is cooked.
3. Place the spaetzle in a serving dish with bits of butter and sprinkle with dill weed.

Serve warm with sour cream, yogurt, or Parmesan cheese, or serve the spaetzle with Herbed Goulash spooned over it. Spaetzle is also great in soup or broth.

Serves 4–6

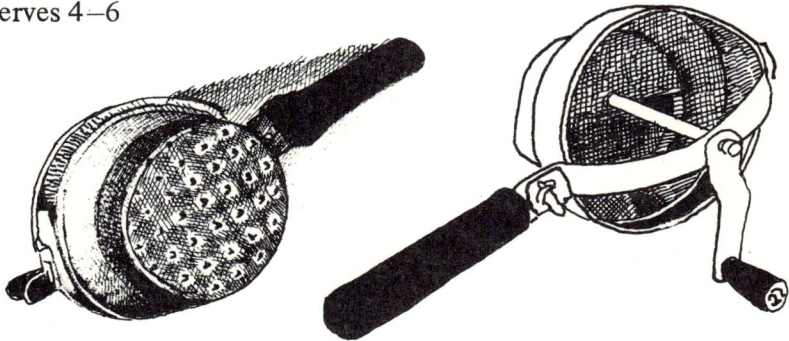

Kasha Varnishkes

Our friend Vladimir Ussachevasky, electronic music composer, arrived at our house late one evening after a hectic day of giving lectures downstate and a long bus ride to Trumansburg. With only a hot dog to tide him over, he was extremely hungry. As I was about to serve dinner, a friend called me long distance to tell me about her impending divorce. Obviously, I couldn't tell her to call me back. The conversation took some time, and after it was over, I needed a bit more time to recover my balance.

The meal was delayed an hour in all. I felt a bit sheepish at having kept him waiting so long, but breathed more easily when I saw his face light up when the kasha was served. After three heaping platefuls, he no longer remembered the delay.

Kasha is another name for buckwheat groats. When cooked with egg, salt and water, it puffs up and becomes very light. Traditionally, bow noodles and fried onions are mixed in with the cooked kasha. The groats come in three grinds, but I prefer them whole.

My parents are Roumanian, and we ate this often at home. It's a fine replacement for starch and makes an interesting change of pace from potatoes or pasta. It is also extremely nutritious.

> 1 egg, beaten
> 1 cup buckwheat groats
> 1 t salt
> 1/4 cup shortening
> 2 cups water
> 3 or 4 large onions, chopped and fried
>   until brown in oil or chicken fat
> 2 cups uncooked bow noodles

1. Melt the shortening in a large fry pan.
2. Combine the egg, groats and salt. Stir into the fry pan. Mix for about a minute.
3. Add water and bring to a boil. Cook, tightly covered, over low heat until all water is absorbed, about 15 minutes. The

groats should be fluffy.

4. Cook the noodles until done but not mushy.

5. Mix together the groats, noodles and sauteed onions and gently toss.

Try this recipe as a stuffing for turkey.

Serves 4–6

Onion Patch Pudding

This pudding consists of a biscuit dough layer topped by onion, egg and parsley, with a sour cream topping. The result is a custard–like puffed topping which complements the onion bread inside.

>   2 cups chopped onion
>   1/2 cup butter
>   3 eggs
>   1 T parsley
>   salt
>   pepper
>   2 cups sifted flour
>   3 t baking powder
>   dill weed
>   3/4 cup milk
>   1/2 cup sour cream or yogurt

1. Saute the onions in 1/4 cup of butter and cool.

2. Combine 1 egg, beaten, with the parsley and 1/2 teaspoon salt and 1/8 teaspoon pepper. Add the sauteed onion.

3. Sift together the flour and baking powder and 1 teaspoon salt. Cut in 1/4 cup butter until the particles are fine. Then add the milk and blend.

4. Knead the dough on a floured board 10–12 times. Pat into a 9" square pan. Spread the onion mixture over the dough.

5. Combine the sour cream (or yogurt), 2 eggs, 1/2 teaspoon salt and 1/8 teaspoon pepper. Beat, and pour over the dough and onions. Sprinkle with dill weed.

6. Bake at 375° for 35–40 minutes, or until brown.

Serves 6

Oven Baked Brown Rice With 4 Variations

Even my daughter Laura, who doesn't like rice, likes this dish.
It is tasty and nutritious, and every grain is separate. Use long
grain rice. Short grain rice takes much longer and is more mushy.

        3 cups uncooked brown rice
        6 1/2 cups chicken stock, or 6 chicken
                bouillon cubes with 6 1/2 cups
                cold water
        3 T butter or margarine
        1 t ground allspice
        1/2 t ground cinnamon
        salt and pepper
        3/4 cup raisins

1. Mix all the ingredients together and spread in a flat baking
dish, about 10" x 15". Cover tightly with foil.
2. Bake in a 350° oven for 50 minutes, or until all the liquid is
absorbed and the grains separate when fluffed with a fork.
    Stir briefly with a fork before serving.

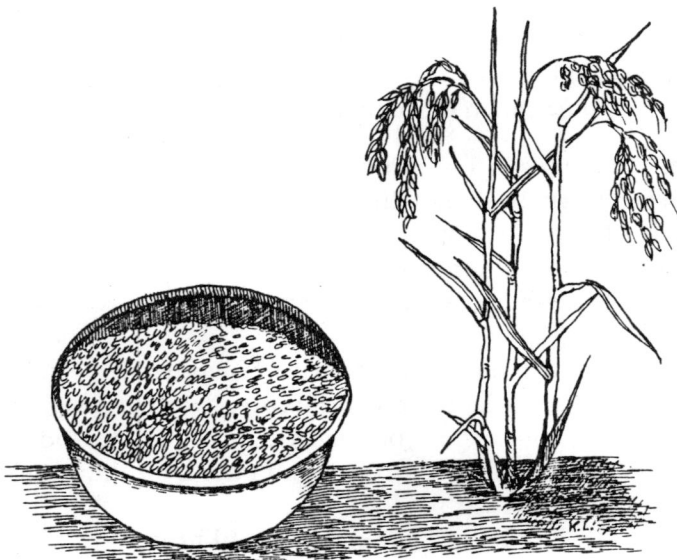

Variation 1

Do not bake the raisins with the rice. When rice is done, add sauteed raisins, nuts and spices as follows:

1 small onion, diced
3 T butter
1/2 cup raisins
1 t chili powder
4 T slivered almonds

1. Melt the butter and add chili powder and onions. Saute until the onions are golden.
2. Add the remaining ingredients and saute another 3—5 minutes.
3. Mix into the cooked rice.

Variation 2

Omit the raisins, chili and almonds from above and use fried onions and curry powder instead.

Variation 3

Use beef broth in place of the chicken stock for a heavier flavor.

Variation 4

Saute onions, mushrooms, and pepper (use bacon fat if possible) and fold into the cooked rice. Omit the raisins, nuts and spices.

Serves 6—8

Cooked Vegetables & Fruit
Stir Fry Vegetables Shirleigh

In 1975 Moog and I spent two delightful weeks in Nyon, Switzerland, where the Polymoog had its first field test on Patrick Moraz's record "I". We shared a large villa with all the musicians, each of us having our own bedrooms but sharing living room, kitchen and swimming pool. There was a grand selection of vegetables at the local markets and I had time to play. The dish I made most, which is still a family favorite, was Stir-Fry Vegetables Shirleigh. You may make this with any combination of vegetables that pleases you. In a pinch, I use frozen mixed vegetables as a base and then add whatever fresh vegetables I have on hand.

The method here is important—the ingredients and the amounts are variable.

    1 clove garlic
    1 medium zucchini, sliced into small chunks
    3 onions, cut in rings
    6 carrots, peeled and sliced on the diagonal
    2 stalks broccoli, cut in pieces
    1 cup snow peas
    1/4—1/2 lb mushrooms, sliced
    1 cup bean sprouts
    2 cups spinach, or Swiss chard
    2 cups celery pieces and leaves
    1 cup string beans
    2 cups Chinese cabbage
    1 green pepper, cut in long strips
    1/3 cup olive oil, peanut oil, butter or a
            combination of any 2
    dash of pepper
    a pinch of oregano and basil
    half a tomato
    grated Parmesan cheese
    1 or 2 T soy sauce

1. Saute the garlic in the oil. Add the pepper, basil and oregano.
2. Add the vegetables which require the longest cooking time
and stir until they are just about done.
3. Add the quick cooking vegetables, the soy sauce and the half
tomato, squeezed so that it is seedless. Also add a sprinkle of
grated cheese.
4. Cook until all the vegetables are done, but still crunchy.

Sprinkle with more grated cheese before serving.

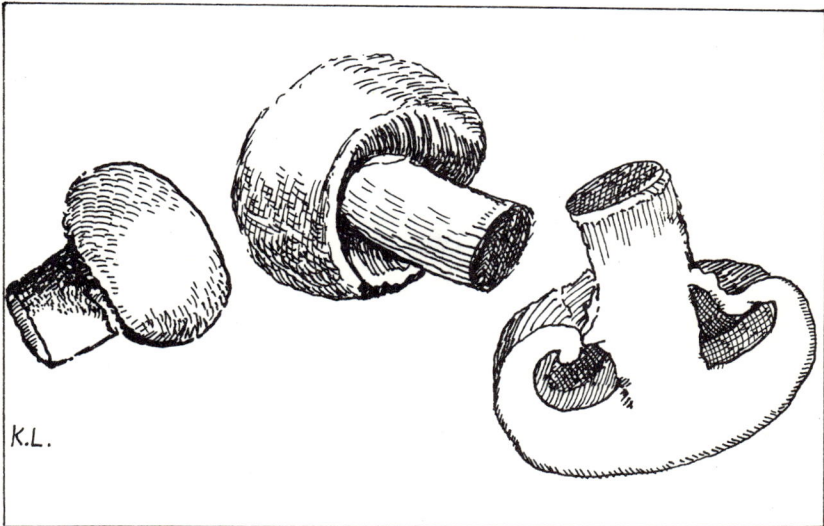

K.L.

STEAMED VEGETABLES

I think the nicest thing to happen to vegetables lately is the wide distribution of stainless steel vegetable steamers costing $3.00–$4.00. They fit into a large soup pot or frying pan. I use a large frying pan with a Dutch oven cover for everything except cauliflower and cabbage. These require the bottom of a Dutch oven, instead of a frying pan.

With a steamer, vegetables cook quickly without being immersed in water. The vegetables with crunch retain it. I have yet to find a vegetable I couldn't cook beautifully with a steamer. Any water left over can be saved in the refrigerator for soup stock. Be careful with the cabbage family. These vegetables have strong juices, and you should be discriminating when you use them for soup.

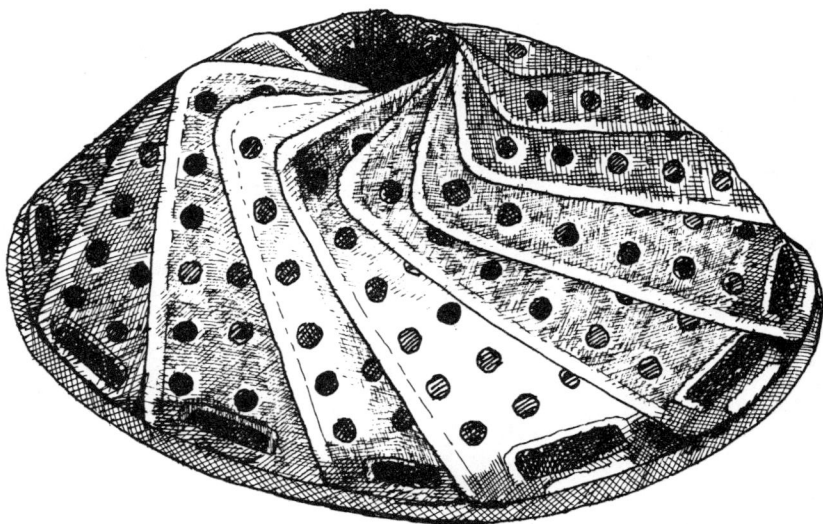

Broccoli With Cheese Sauce

This is one of those dishes that are much better than the component parts, in a word—synergistic!

4 large stalks or 1 bunch broccoli
2 T butter
2 T flour
pepper to taste
1 cup warm milk
1/2—3/4 cup grated cheese

1. Steam broccoli.
2. Melt the butter over low heat and mix in the flour. Then add warm milk and stir with a whisk. Cook for a few minutes. The mixture should be smooth and thick.
3. Grind in a bit of pepper. Add the cheese and mix again until all is blended and smooth.
4. Line a platter with broccoli, alternating flower and stem ends. Pour cheese sauce down the center of the platter. Serve and watch it disappear.

Serves 4

Dilled Carrots In Orange Butter

When my children were young, I found out that they liked jazzed up vegetables much more than plain boiled vegetables and butter.

> 6—8 carrots, cut into slices on the diagonal
> 1/8 lb butter
> 1/2 orange, using the juice, pulp, and grated rind
> 1/2 t dill weed

1. Cook carrots in a small amount of water or steam them.
2. While the carrots are cooking, melt the butter and add the dill and orange juice, pulp and rind.
3. Drain the carrots. The liquid can be saved for soup stock. Place the carrots in the butter mixture and mix thoroughly.

Serves 6

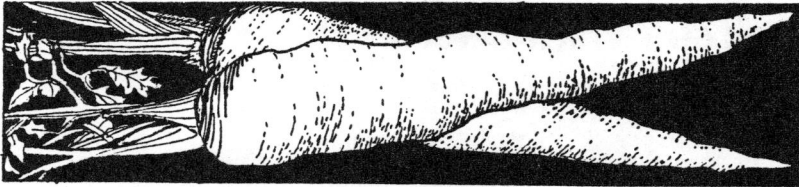

String Beans In Lemon Butter With Toasted Almonds

> 1·1/2 lb string beans
> 1/8 lb butter
> 1/2 cup slivered almonds, toasted
> 1/2 lemon, juice and pulp

1. Steam string beans until just done.
2. Melt butter and add lemon juice and pulp.
3. Drain the beans, reserving the juice for stock.
4. Mix beans and lemon butter.
5. Toast almonds under broiler. Sprinkle on string beans just before serving.

Serves 4—6

Ratatouille

Rat-a-two-e is a vegetable melange of eggplant, zucchini, tomato, pepper and onion, sprinkled with a lot of tasty things and baked in the oven. Traditionally cooked, it calls for many pans and fussing. This version is super easy, calling for just one bowl.

Ratatouille may be eaten hot or cold. When the garden produce begins to roll in, I make huge casseroles and keep it in the frig. It is a very tasty, low calorie nibble. When I make too much to eat within one week, I freeze it in cottage cheese containers (2 lb size) and use it throughout the winter.

Frozen ratatouille may become soupy after it has been thawed. Sprinkle the top with bread crumbs and grated Parmesan cheese before baking to absorb excess fluid. Put a pat of butter on top and broil till bubbly.

> 1 small eggplant
> 3 or 4 medium zucchini
> 1 green pepper
> 1 large onion
> 3 tomatoes
> 2 T sugar
> basil (about 1/2 t)
> oregano (about 1/2 t)
> 1/3 cup olive oil
> 2 cloves garlic, minced
> 1 1/2 t salt

1. Cut eggplant and zucchini into 1" cubes.
2. Place in a 3 quart casserole and drizzle with half the oil mix (olive oil, minced garlic and salt).
3. Cut pepper and onion into thin strips. Place on top of ingredients in a bowl and drizzle with the rest of the oil mix.
4. Cover and bake 45 minutes to 1 hour.
5. Peel and slice 3 tomatoes. Arrange the tomatoes on top of the baked vegetables and sprinkle with sugar, basil and oregano.
6. Bake uncovered 15 minutes longer. Serve hot or cold.
I usually make a double batch, using 2 bowls.

Curried Fruit Bake

Peaches, pears and pineapple baked in a curry butter make grand partners for pork, lamb or chicken.

1 large can peach halves, drained
1 No. 2 can pineapple slices, drained
1 large can pear halves, drained
1/3 cup butter, melted
1/2 cup brown sugar
3 t curry powder.

1. Arrange the fruits attractively in a 1 1/2 quart ovenproof dish or casserole.
2. Add the brown sugar and curry to the melted butter and spoon over the fruit.
3. Bake at 325 degrees for 45 minutes, uncovered.

If you buy fruits packed in juice rather than heavy syrup, you can use the drained juices to make a juice melange for the children. Just add a bit of lemon juice and water to balance the tastes.

Salads & Dressings
Feta Cheese Salad

This is a tomato season special. The salty cheese, the sun ripened tomatoes and the basil are a great combination. Don't tamper with this recipe too much.

> 5—6 medium size tomatoes, cut in wedges
> 1/2 lb feta cheese, crumbled
> 1 T basil
> 1/3 cup olive oil
> 2 lemons, juice and pulp
> 1—2 t Dijon mustard
> 1/4 cup celery, stalks and leaves, chopped
> or spinach leaves torn in half, optional

1. Place tomatoes in a bowl and sprinkle feta cheese and basil over them.

2. Combine olive oil, lemon juice, lemon pulp and mustard to make a salad dressing.

3. Pour the dressing over all and toss gently.

Black Greek olives are good with this, served on the side.

Serves 4

Spinach Salad

This is my favorite salad. It requires three simple ingredients for the salad and three more for the dressing.

    1 bag spinach
    1/2 lb bacon, cooked and crumbled
            (save 2 T of the grease)
    12 oz fresh mushrooms, cleaned and sliced
            in crosswise slices
    3/4 cup heavy cream
    1 1/2 t fresh lemon juice
    1/2–3/4 t Dijon mustard

1. Tear the washed spinach leaves into salad size pieces. Discard the large stems.
2. Toss with crumbled bacon, mushrooms, and 2 T of the warm bacon fat.
3. Mix the cream, mustard and lemon juice quickly, in that order.
4. Pour the dressing over the salad and toss.

Serves 4–6

Cracked Wheat Salad

There is nothing more delicious in summer than this lemony, minty wheat salad, served ice cold.

    1 cup cracked wheat (bulghur), see page 71
    2 cups chicken stock, homemade or made
            from bouillon cubes
    1/4 cup mint leaves, finely chopped or 2 T
            dried mint leaves
    1 onion, chopped fine
    1 cup parsley, finely chopped (Italian parsley
            if possible) or 2 T dried parsley
    2 cucumbers, skinned and diced
    2 lemons, juice and pulp
    olive oil and salt to taste

1. Pour boiling chicken broth or bouillon over wheat and let soak for two hours or until wheat absorbs all the fluid.
2. Add mint, parsley, onions and cucumbers. If you use dried mint and parsley, add them to the wheat before you soak it.
3. Add olive oil, lemon juice and salt to taste.
4. Toss and serve cold.

Tomato sections may be added when they are in season. Add a pinch of basil along with the tomatoes.

Serves 6

Black Radish Salad

This is my father's idea of a salad. I told Moog about it so often, he said, "If you ever find those black radishes at the market, buy one and let me see what your dad likes so well." I did find them at my supermarket and I made the salad. Wouldn't you know, Moog loved it.

Whenever we can, we grow black radishes in our garden, both the round ones for the fall and the long ones for spring. They look like small black turnips.

1 radish
salt to taste
olive oil to taste
grated carrot, optional

1. Peel radish and cut in half for easier handling.
2. Grate on coarse grater.
3. Add olive oil and salt to taste. Toss and serve.

Serves 2—4

Carrot Salad With 2 Variations

Most people think that greens are the basis of a salad. However, there are other possibilities, among them carrot salad. It has a lovely color and moreover is tasty and good for you.

>   5—8 large carrots
>   1/3 cup olive oil
>   1 lemon, juice and pulp
>   1 t Dijon mustard

1. Grate the carrots coarsely.
2. You may add any other vegetable you wish, but let the carrots predominate. Chopped celery stalks and leaves, radishes, peppers, cucumbers or greens are some possibilities.
3. Mix the olive oil, lemon juice, lemon pulp and mustard in a cup.
4. Pour over salad. Toss and eat.

Variation 1—Carrot—Tuna Salad

Add a can of tuna, flaked with a fork, and a jar of artichoke hearts, along with the oil in the jar. Throw a bit of oregano into the dressing. This carrot—tuna salad is a meal in itself when served with bran muffins or a good bread.

Variation 2—Grated Carrot Waldorf

>   5—8 large carrots, grated
>   apple pieces
>   raisins
>   nuts
>   orange pieces
>   mayonnaise

Mix all the fruits and nuts together in a proportion that pleases you. You can either mix mayonnaise in or serve with the mayonnaise on top.

Serves 4—6

Olive Celery Salad

You very often see this salad in delicatessen display counters. It's very easy to make yourself. The olives and oregano give a nice bite and a lot of personality to the celery. Buy salad olives for this salad—they are cheaper than whole olives.

2 cups chopped celery and celery leaves
1 cup olives in pieces
1 clove garlic, finely minced
2 T olive juice
olive oil to taste
1 t oregano

Mix all ingredients together in a bowl and let set for about an hour before serving. This can be stored in the refrigerator for about a week.

Serves 4—6

Cole Slaw

I am particularly fond of this slaw. It's tasty, and it keeps for about a week in the refrigerator.

1 head cabbage, shredded
1 onion, chopped fine
2 green bell peppers, chopped fine
10—12 stuffed olives, sliced
1/2 cup sugar
3/4 cup white or cider vinegar
1 t salt
1 t celery seed
1 t prepared mustard
1/8 t black pepper
1/2 cup salad oil

1. Combine cabbage, onion, peppers and olives in a bowl.
2. Mix the remaining ingredients in a small saucepan. Bring to a boil and cook 2—3 minutes.
3. Pour over the cabbage.
4. Cover and let stand in the refrigerator 6—12 hours.

Serves 8—12

Tossed Salad

I guess I should give you a good start on the options for tossed salad. It's really a free form on which you can impose your own personality. Vary the ingredients with the seasons or your moods. There are so many tastes and textures available that you should always experiment.

Greens (usually the base)

> lettuce
> beet greens
> Swiss chard
> spinach
> parsley
> dill
> Chinese cabbage
> celery leaves

The Rest

> tomatoes
> cucumbers
> peppers
> carrots
> celery stalks
> onion rings
> mushrooms
> peas
> raisins

> cooked chick peas
> nuts
> artichoke hearts
> avacados
> apples
> grated hard boiled egg
> summer squash
> cheese (bleu, Cheddar, Parmesan, Swiss or feta)

Some very special combinations are basil, tomatoes and mustard; and dill, garlic slivers and chick peas.

Grated hard boiled egg makes a lacy topping. When you mix it into the salad, it merges with the dressing to give a very smooth, special taste.

For a dressing, I recommend Moog House dressing, recipe on following page. Be sure your vegetables are washed but patted dry before you add the dressing.

Shirleigh's Favorite Italian Dressing

    3/4 cup olive oil
    1 or 2 garlic cloves, minced
    1 t oregano
    lemon, juice and pulp
    salt and pepper to taste
    1/2 t Dijon mustard

Mix all ingredients in a jar and shake vigorously. Store in the refrigerator.

Makes 1 cup

Moog House Dressing

This dressing has, for our family, just the right blend of tart lemon, bland oil and sharp mustard. I hope you like it too.

    1 cup olive oil
    1 cup peanut oil
    2–3 t soy sauce
    juice and pulp of 1 lemon
    2 t Dijon mustard
    1 clove garlic, slivered

Combine all the ingredients in a jar and shake vigorously. Store in the refrigerator and use as needed.

Makes 2 1/2 cups

Blender Mayonnaise With 2 Variations

Making mayonnaise in a blender is a lead pipe cinch. Once you realize how easy it is and how superior it is to any commercial mayo, you'll be hooked. It's also nice to know that, if you have eggs and oil on hand, you can always make mayonnaise. It's useful to make a double batch and store half in the refrigerator.

> 1 egg
> 1 t salt
> 1 t sugar
> 1/2 t mustard
> 1/4 t paprika
> 3 T lemon juice with pulp
> 1 1/2 cups salad oil

1. Put all the ingredients except the oil into blender and blend for just a few seconds. Uncover.
2. Add the oil in a slow thin thread with the blender running. When the mixture becomes very thick and smooth, turn off the motor and mix the mayo from the bottom to the top. Continue adding the oil as the motor runs, until all the oil is incorporated.

Variation 1—Green Mayonnaise

Add 1 clove garlic, 1/2 to 1 cup parsley and a dash of Tabasco. The mayonnaise is laden with parsley for color and flavor. The garlic and Tabasco give it a subtle zip.

Variation 2—Curried Mayonnaise

For each cup of mayonnaise, add 1 or 2 teaspoons curry powder. This dressing is a zesty way to perk up a salad. It also makes a fine dip for a fresh vegetable platter.

Makes 1 1/2—2 cups

Breads, Spreads & Dips

Breads, Spreads & Dips

† **Easy recipes for the inexperienced hostess.**

‡ **These recipes can be frozen.**

Cornbread

This cornbread is chockfull of things that are good for you, and it is delicious besides.

> 1 cup coarse yellow cornmeal
> 1/2 cup white flour
> 1/2 cup whole wheat flour
> 2–3 T powdered milk
> 4 t baking powder
> 1 1/2 t salt
> 1 cup milk or buttermilk or 1/2 cup
>   yogurt and 1/2 cup water
> 1 egg
> 2 T oil or bacon fat
> 2–3 T wheat germ
> 2 T honey (optional)

1. Preheat oven to 425°.
2. Put all the dry ingredients in a bowl and mix together.
3. Add all the wet ingredients and mix till uniformly moist.
4. Put all the batter into a greased 8″ x 8″ pan. I like to bake corn bread in my cast iron skillet, greased with some tasty bacon fat. I warm the skillet in the oven while I mix the batter. When I'm ready, I pour the batter into the hot skillet. Bake 20–25 minutes, until golden brown. Serve warm.

Makes one 8″ x 8″ loaf

Muffins With 3 Variations

Muffins are good to eat and whip up fast. The batter should be mixed until the dry ingredients are just dampened. It will probably be lumpy. Don't try to beat the lumps out.

> 2 cups sifted flour
> 1/4 cup sugar
> 1 T baking powder
> 1 t salt
> 1 egg
> 1 cup milk
> 1/4 cup melted butter or oil

1. Preheat oven to 400°, and grease 12 muffin cups.
2. Sift together the flour, sugar, baking powder and salt into a large bowl.
3. Make a well in the center of the dry ingredients and add egg, milk and butter or oil. Stir just enough to moisten the dry ingredients.
4. Fill the greased muffin cups 2/3 full.
5. Bake 20 minutes, or until the muffins are golden brown. Loosen the muffins with a spatula to remove them from the pan. Serve warm or at room temperature.

Variation 1—Jam Muffins

Fill the muffin cups half full with batter. Spoon into each cup 1 teaspoon of your favorite jam. Add more batter to make the cups 2/3 full.

Variation 2—Bacon and Cheese Muffins

Half a cup of crumbled bacon and/or grated cheese may be mixed into the batter with the dry ingredients. I prefer Cheddar or Parmesan.

Variation 3—Crumb Muffins

A crumb topping can be sprinkled over the uncooked muffins.
Mix together 1/2 cup brown sugar, 1/3 cup chopped nuts, 1/4
teaspoon ground cinnamon and 1/4 teaspoon ground nutmeg for
an easy, tasty crumb topping.

Makes 12 muffins

Bran Muffins

These wheaty muffins are easy to make. They are good with salads, souffles, soups—whatever. They freeze well and are nifty, split in half, topped with butter and toasted under a broiler for a morning treat.

> 1 1/2 cups bran cereal
> 1 cup milk
> 1 egg
> 1/3 cup oil
> 1 1/2 cup flour
> 1/2 cup sugar
> 3 t baking powder
> 1 t salt
> 1/2 cup raisins, optional

1. Combine bran cereal and milk. Let stand 2 minutes until most of the milk is absorbed.
2. Add the egg and oil. Beat well.
3. Sift together flour, sugar, baking powder and salt. Add to the bran mixture, stirring only until ingredients are combined. Add raisins if you want them. Stir gently.
4. Fill 2 1/2'' muffin cups three quarters full.
5. Bake in a moderate oven (375°) 25 minutes or until muffins are lightly browned.

Makes 12—16

Whole Wheat Rolls

These are do-all rolls. They are the right size for hamburgers and sandwiches. They are also just fine served on their own with butter or jam. I usually make a double batch and freeze what I don't use.

> 1 T dry yeast (1 pkg)
> 2 T honey
> 1 1/2 cups warm milk, preferable buttermilk
> 5 T corn oil
> 1 egg
> 1 t salt
> 4—5 cups flour, half whole wheat,
>   half unbleached white

1. Mix yeast, honey and buttermilk or milk. Let sit 5 minutes.
2. Add oil, egg and salt. Mix.
3. Add flour and mix.
4. Knead about 5 minutes. Let rise 1 hour.
5. Shape into rolls by rolling the dough out 3/4" thick and cutting circles out. Use a large round cookie cutter or a large, floured drinking glass.
6. Place on greased cookie sheets. Let rise 20 minutes.
7. Bake in preheated 350° oven 15—20 minutes.

Sticky Buns

These are the classic, sticky breakfast buns, full of nuts and spices. I usually double the recipe and fill two or three pie pans full of buns. I bake all the buns. What I don't use immediately I cover tightly with foil and freeze. When I am ready to use them, they can be heated in the same pie pan.

> 1/2 cup lukewarm milk
> 1 t salt
> 1 T sugar
> 1 T dry yeast
> 1 egg
> 3 T oil
> 1 1/2 cups flour
> butter, in small pieces
> honey, brown sugar or maple syrup
> cinnamon
> raisins
> nuts (walnuts, pecans, or sunflower kernels)

1. Mix together the first 4 ingredients and then stir in the next 3 ingredients. Knead this dough on a floured board 6–10 times.
2. Roll the dough into a rectangle approximately 10" x 15". Sprinkle with the butter, brown sugar (or honey, or maple syrup), cinnamon, raisins and nuts.
3. Roll the dough up lengthwise and cut in two. Cut each half into 9 pieces.
4. Grease a 9" pie pan or cake pan with melted butter and sprinkle sugar and nuts over the butter.
5. Place the rolls in the pan, cut side down, and let rise for 20–30 minutes.
6. Drizzle maple syrup or honey over the rolls and bake at 350° for 20–30 minutes.
7. Invert on a plate while still hot. Serve warm or cold.

Makes 18 buns

Popovers

Popovers are light, buttery, souffle-like muffins. They are hollow in the middle, thereby allowing room for the butter to melt. They are magical to make—people light up when their popovers "pop."

I have made popovers many times. The only thing that is absolutely essential is that the butter be melted, bubbling hot but not burning, in the muffin cups before the batter is poured in. The popover batter will then begin to cook as soon as it touches the pan. My method is to put a pat of butter in each muffin section. I then put the tin in the oven. When the butter bubbles slightly, I take the muffin pan out of the oven, place it on the open oven door and pour the batter right on the spot.

    1/4 t salt
    1 cup flour
    1 cup milk
    2 eggs
    1 T butter, melted

1. Sift together flour and salt.
2. Beat the eggs with beater. Add milk and butter.
3. Sift the flour into the egg and milk mixture. Beat just enough to make a smooth batter.
4. Fill hot buttered muffin cups about 1/3 full.
5. Bake in a 350° oven 45 minutes to 1 hour until popovers are puffed and golden brown. *Don't open the oven door while the popovers are baking.*
6. The muffins should lift out easily. If they are obstinate, a spatula will ease them out.
7. Serve right away with butter.

Makes 12 popovers

Cheese Bread

I've been making this for years. It is easy and delicious. Wonderful toasted and slathered with butter and tomato jam.

> 1 cup milk
> 3 T sugar
> 1 T salt
> 1 T shortening
> 2 pkg dry yeast
> 1 cup warm water
> 1 cup grated Cheddar cheese
> 4 1/2 cups sifted flour

1. Scald milk, sugar, salt and shortening. Let stand until luke warm.

2. In a large bowl, dissolve yeast in 1 cup warm water. Add milk mixture, grated cheese and flour. Mix well.

3. Cover batter with Saran Wrap and a heavy dish towel. Set in a warm place free from drafts until batter doubles in bulk, about 45 minutes.

4. Stir batter down. Beat 1/2 minute with wooden spoon. Turn into greased 1 1/2 quart casserole or 2 5" x 9" loaf pans.

5. Bake uncovered at 375 degrees for 1 hour.

I prefer one big loaf baked in a casserole. It looks festive and tastes great. Lovely, teamed with port wine jelly or tomato jam.

   Try adding a tablespoon of dill or fresh minced parsley for variety.

Makes 2 5" x 9" loaves or 1 large round loaf

Herb Bread

This half wheat bread is liberally sprinkled with tasty herbs.
The final product is a delicate, tasty braided loaf.

> 4 1/2—5 cups of flour, half white and
> half whole wheat
> 2 pkg dry yeast
> 1 1/2 t dill weed
> 1 t caraway seed
> 1/2 t celery seed
> 3/4 cup milk
> 3/4 cup water
> 2 T shortening
> 2 T sugar
> 2 t salt
> 2 medium size eggs or 1 large egg

1. In a large mixing bowl, stir together 1 3/4 cups flour, the yeast and all the herbs.
2. Combine in a saucepan the milk, water, shortening, sugar and salt. Heat to 120°—130°, and then pour it into the dry mixture.
3. Add the egg to the above mixture and beat at low speed for half a minute. Beat at high speed for 3 minutes more.
4. Gradually stir in enough of the remaining flour to make a soft dough. Knead on a floured surface for 10—15 minutes.
5. Divide the dough into quarters and roll the quarters into long ropes. To make the braids, twist two ropes together on a greased cookie sheet and press the ends under to seal Repeat for second braid.
6. Let rise until double in bulk. This should take 30 or 40 minutes.
7. Bake at 350° for 20—30 minutes.

Makes 2 loaves

Garlic Bread

Real garlic bread is so easy to make; don't settle for anything less.

1 long, slim loaf of Italian bread slashed
      crosswise every 1 1/2". Don't
      cut all the way through the loaf;
      leave the slices attached.
1/4 lb unsalted butter
4—8 cloves of garlic, finely minced
enough aluminum foil to wrap the bread

1. Melt the butter over medium heat and saute the garlic in it. Cook the garlic until it is yellow and soft, but not brown.
2. Spread the garlic butter in between each slice of bread, and pour any remaining garlic butter over the top of the bread.
3. Split the loaf into two sections and wrap each section with foil. Heat in a 350° oven for 15 or 20 minutes. Serve the bread hot, one section at a time. If you have one of those long, woven baskets, now is the time to use it.

Variation: Cheese—Herb—Garlic Bread

For a tasty variation on garlic bread, add 2 teaspoons each of parsley and oregano to the melted butter and garlic, and sprinkle some grated Parmesan cheese in between each slice.

Zucchini Bread

In the summer, when the zucchini boom is on, I grate zucchini and freeze it in 2 cup portions. When I am ready to make this bread, I thaw the zucchini and use the watery part as well as the pulp.

    4 eggs
    2 cups sugar, 1/2 white, 1/2 brown
    1 cup vegetable oil
    3 1/2 cups unbleached flour
    1 1/2 t baking soda
    1 1/2 t salt
    1 t cinnamon
    3/4 t baking powder
    2 cups grated zucchini
    1 cup chopped nuts
    1 cup raisins
    1 t vanilla

1. Beat the eggs.
2. Add the sugar gradually, beating as you go.
3. Add the oil.
4. Combine the flour, baking soda, salt, cinnamon and baking powder.
5. Add dry ingredients to the egg mixture alternately with the grated zucchini.
6. Stir in the chopped nuts, vanilla and raisins. You may substitute another cup of raisins for the cup of chopped nuts.
7. Bake in greased and floured loaf pans at 350°, 55–65 minutes. The loaves freeze well.

Makes 2 loaves

Spreads

Tomato Jam

This jam is a favorite of Richard Teitelbaum, a long time friend, composer, and performer of electronic music. He almost always carries away a jar with him when he leaves. It is spiced with cinnamon and cloves, and has the tang of lemon. The lemon slices in the jam crystallize and make it even more special.

> 2 1/4 lbs fully ripe tomatoes (3 cups chopped tomatoes)
> 2 lemons, cut in thin slices and seeds removed
> 6 1/2 cups sugar
> 1 bottle Certo pectin
> 1 t cinnamon
> 1/2 t ground cloves
> 6—8 whole cloves

1. Prepare the tomatoes by dropping them in boiling water briefly. Peel and chop them.
2. Put them in a pan and bring to a boil. Simmer 10 minutes.
3. Measure 3 cups of prepared tomatoes into a large saucepan and add lemon slices, sugar and spices. Mix well.
4. Bring to a full rolling boil over high heat and boil for 1 minute, stirring constantly.
5. Remove from heat and stir in the pectin. Skim off the foam with a metal spoon. Stir and skim for 5 minutes to cool the mixture and prevent the fruit from floating.
6. Ladle into sterilized jars and cover with 1/2" hot paraffin.

Variation—Apple—Ginger Jam

1. Use 2 cups tomatoes, scalded, peeled and chopped.
2. Add 1 1/2—2 cups apples, peeled and chopped. Place tomatoes and apples in a pan and bring to a boil.
3. Omit the spices above (cinnamon and cloves; use candied ginger instead). Follow directions above from step 4 on.

Makes about 7 cups of jam

Port Wine Jelly

This is a lovely winey jelly that is super simple to make. It is great at lunch or supper; on muffins, popovers, pancakes, etc. It is a real eye opener in the morning on toast. It's also special enough to be used as an elegant Christmas gift.

If your double boiler is large enough, this recipe can be doubled easily.

>   2 cups port wine
>   3 cups sugar
>   1/2 bottle Certo fruit pectin

1. Mix the wine and sugar together in the top part of a double boiler. The bottom part should contain enough water to reach the bottom of the top pan.
2. Bring to a boil and stir until all the sugar is dissolved. This will take 5—8 minutes.
3. Remove from the heat and immediately stir in the Certo.
4. Pour into sterilized glasses. Cover with 1/8" hot paraffin.

Makes 5 medium size glasses

Red Pepper Jam

This jam is lovely with lunch or dinner. It tastes fine on cream cheese.

> 2 cups sweet red peppers, chopped
> 1 t salt
> 5 1/2 cups sugar
> 1 1/4 cups cider vinegar
> 1 bottle liquid pectin
> 4—6 shakes of Tabasco sauce

1. Grind peppers in a food grinder or blender. The grind should be fine, but do not make a puree.
2. Add salt and let stand for several hours. Drain, discard liquid.
3. Combine all ingredients except pectin in a saucepan, and bring to a full boil. Remove from heat and set aside for 15—20 minutes.
4. Return to heat and bring to a full rolling boil. Boil for 2 minutes.
5. Remove from heat and add pectin. Stir.
6. Skim off the foam, and pour the jam into sterilized jelly glasses.
7. Cover with a thin layer of liquid paraffin.

Makes 6—7 cups of jam

Freezer Strawberry Jam

This is a jam that is stored frozen, rather than cooked and preserved. It is the best recipe I know for preserving the fresh taste of strawberries.

> 1 1/2 cups cleaned and sliced strawberries
> 4 cups sugar
> 2 T lemon juice
> 1/2 bottle Certo pectin

1. Thoroughly crush berries, one layer at a time. Measure 1 1/2 cups into a bowl. Add sugar and mix well.
2. Combine lemon juice and Certo in small bowl and mix.
3. Add to fruit and sugar mixture and stir for 3 minutes. Most sugar crystals will dissolve by that time.
4. Pour quickly into clean freezer containers.
5. Cover with tight lid and allow to sit at room temperature for up to 24 hours until set.
6. Store in the freezer or refrigerator for immediate use.

Sometimes this jam does not set very thick. The amount of pectin in the berries varies with ripeness and the variety of strawberries. You have two choices, maybe three. 1. Boil it up as you eat it 2. use it on ice cream as a super sauce or 3. use it spread thinly on bread. Most of the time the recipe works. The jam is well worth taking the chance. This method works well also with raspberry and peach jam. Consult the Certo recipe book.

Sherried Cheese Spread

Sherry, mustard and cayenne pepper spice up this homemade cheese spread. It's an unusual gift to bring with you when you are invited for dinner, in place of the more prosaic bottle of wine.

    1 lb sharp Cheddar cheese
    1/2 cup dry sherry
    1/4 cup evaporated milk or heavy cream
    1/4 cup butter
    2 t prepared mustard
    1 t salt
    1/8 t cayenne pepper

1. Grate cheese.
2. Add the other ingredients to the grated cheese and mix until smooth and creamy in an electric mixer.

Makes about 3 cups

Chopped Chicken Liver Spread

This is a favorite with just about everyone. When you buy whole chickens to cook for dinner, the livers can be frozen and saved until you have enough of them to make a batch of this recipe.

  1 lb chicken livers
  4 hard boiled eggs
  2 large onions, sliced
  1 clove garlic, minced
  dash of cayenne or ground black pepper
  salt to taste
  1/4–1/2 cup mayonnaise
  6 T butter

1. Melt the butter in a skillet and saute onions and garlic until they are golden brown.
2. Add the chicken livers and fry until the livers are cooked through but are not dry. Cool.
3. Put the liver and onion mixture through a food chopper. Then put the hard boiled eggs through the food chopper (or chop them finely by hand).
4. Mix together the liver, eggs, and mayonnaise. Add salt and pepper to taste.

This spread is nice served on cocktail rye bread or crackers. It's also toothsome in a good rye bread sandwich with lettuce and Bermuda onion

Here are some tasty variations for this recipe: 1. Grind some parsley with the liver. 2. Add a dash of vermouth or sherry. 3. Use bacon fat in place of the butter and put in some crumbled bacon.

Serves 6–10

Dips
Yogurt Tahini

The acid taste of the yogurt and lemon juice in this dip make it most refreshing for a summer dip or salad dressing.

> 2/3 cup yogurt
> 1/3 cup tahini
> 1 lemon, juice and pulp
> fresh ground pepper

Mix the first three ingredients together. Add pepper to taste.

Serves 6

Chick Pea Dip Or Spread

If you serve this as a spread with whole grain bread, the combination of bean and grain will give you a complete protein. It is also lovely served as a dip surrounded by fresh vegetables—cauliflower, carrots, celery, pepper strips, zucchini slices.

> 1 large can chick peas (garbanzos)
> 3 onions, chopped
> 2 T peanut oil or butter
> 1 T sesame seed paste (tahini)
> 2—3 minced garlic cloves
> 1 T smooth peanut butter
> juice & pulp of 1 lemon
> 1 t salt

1. Drain the chick peas and reserve the liquid.
2. Mash the peas with a wooden spoon. Some lumps are okay. They help the texture.
3. Fry the onions and garlic in peanut oil or butter.
4. Add the fried onions, garlic, peanut butter and sesame seed paste, lemon juice and enough of the reserved liquid to the mashed chick peas to get the consistency you like. It should be a little thick if you want to use it as a spread; dips can be thinner.

Serves 6—8

Breads, Spreads, & Dips/147

Chili Con Queso

This is a really boss dip, tasty and hot. It's fine for serving a large crew.

When you seed the peppers wear gloves. The juices can burn the skin.

> 1 large onion, minced
> 1 small clove garlic, minced
> 4 T butter
> 1 lb 13 oz tomatoes, drained
> 4 oz peeled green chili peppers, chopped (make sure all seeds are rinsed off)
> 2 T flour
> 1 cup cream or evaporated milk
> salt to taste
> Tabasco sauce to taste
> 1/2 lb Cheddar or Monterey Jack cheese, finely diced

1. Saute the onion and garlic in 2 T butter until soft.
2. Add tomatoes and simmer till thick. Then add the chilies.
3. Make a white sauce by combining the remaining 2 T butter, flour and cream or evaporated milk. Stir constantly over medium heat until the sauce is thick and smooth.
4. Add the white sauce to the tomatoes and chilies. Season to taste with salt and Tabasco.
5. Just before serving, stir in the cheese and let it melt. Serve in a chafing dish or fondue pot over a sterno flame to keep the dip warm. Corn chips or other sturdy chips should be served with this dip. Potato chips will break.

If you need to prepare this in advance, stop after step 4. The cheese should not be added until you can serve the dip. After you have added the cheese, heat the dip slowly over low heat or a double boiler.

Serves 12

Desserts

Desserts

† **Easy recipes for the inexperienced hostess.**

‡ **These recipes can be frozen.**

Cakes & Pies

I know most big meals are supposed to end with big heavy desserts but it always seems silly to me. People are usually too full but, to be polite, they stuff themselves and feel awful afterward. It's time to call a halt to such foolishness.

I always try to have a light dessert at the end of a big meal. The heavy pies and ultra rich cakes belong at the end of a light meal or at a coffee and cake affair.

Mocha Cream Pie

Small pieces of this pie suffice—It's really rich.

> 9 oz semi-sweet chocolate bits (1 1/2 bags)
> 1 square bitter chocolate
> 4 T hot coffee
> 1 T vanilla
> 2 cups heavy cream, whipped till stiff
> slivered almonds
> 1 baked graham cracker shell

1. Melt together the bitter and semi-sweet chocolate in top of a double boiler.
2. When melted, add hot coffee and stir until smooth. Allow to cool.
3. Add vanilla and mix.
4. Fold the cooled chocolate mixture into the whipped cream.
5. Pour into the pie shell and garnish with almonds. Chill before serving.

Serves 6—8

Ne Plus Ultra Cheesecake

Dick Trythall is a rangy 6' 4" pianist who plays a great deal of modern music. We first met him in Rome and renewed our friendship when he became Creative Associate at S.U.N.Y., Buffalo.

One evening when Dick and his wife Nona were visiting, I made cheesecake for dessert. Dick ate until he could hold no more and proclaimed it the best he'd ever tasted. I believe this is the belle of cheesecakes. It requires care and is expensive, but the taste and texture more than justify the effort.

> 2 1/2 lbs cream cheese
> 1 3/4 cups sugar
> 3 T flour
> 1 1/2 t grated orange rind
> 1 1/2 t grated lemon rind
> 1/4 t vanilla extract
> 7 egg yolks
> 7 egg whites, beaten stiff
> 1/4 cup heavy cream, whipped
> graham cracker pie crust mix

1. Prepare the graham cracker crust according to the package directions and line the bottom and sides of a 9" spring form pan with it.
2. Combine cheese, sugar, flour, grated rinds and vanilla in a mixing bowl. Add egg yolks one at a time, stirring after each addition.
3. Gently fold the whites and cream into the above mixture. Whipping the cream and beating the egg whites separately make this cake as light as possible and free of cracks. The slow cooling process helps keep it from falling and developing a heavy texture.
4. Pour the cheese mixture into the crust and bake in a 450° oven for 10 minutes.
5. Reduce the oven temperature to 300° and continue baking for 1 hour and 20 minutes.

5. Turn off the heat and prop the oven door open with a wooden spoon. Allow the cake to cool in the oven for one hour.

6. Remove the cake to a draft free spot and allow it to cool at room temperature for 1 hour.

7. Refrigerate, and serve cold. You can top the cake with strawberries or blueberries or other fruit, but I have always felt that was gilding the lily. If you want to glaze it, use the recipe for the glaze for Strawberry Nut Torte, or the strawberry glaze recipe that follows.

Serves 12

STRAWBERRY GLAZE

1 1/2 quarts fresh strawberries
1/4 cup sugar
1 T cornstarch
1 T lemon juice

1. Wash, hull and drain the berries.

2. Mash or puree in blender a half quart of the berries.

3. In a small saucepan combine the sugar and cornstarch, mixing well.

4. Stir in the strawberry puree and bring to a boil, stirring over medium heat. Boil for 1 minute, until the mixture is thickened and translucent. Remove from heat and cool slightly.

5. Stir in the lemon juice and cool completely.

6. Arrange the remaining quart of berries over the cooled cheesecake, with the points up. Spoon the glaze over them.

If you cannot get fresh berries, get 2 lbs of frozen whole berries. Drain them and save 3/4 cup of the juice. Mix 2 tablespoons sugar and 1 tablespoon cornstarch into the juice and continue as above.

Banana Kuchen

I often make these kuchen in round aluminum foil pie pans, bake them and let them cool. Then I cover the top with more aluminum foil and pop them in the freezer. Very useful for surprise visits. If I have apples, peaches or plums, I skin and slice them on top of the kuchen, pinwheel fashion, and sprinkle with the topping.

Cake

>1/4 cup butter or margarine
>3/4 cup sugar
>1 egg
>1 medium banana, sliced
>1/4 cup milk
>1 1/2 cups sifted flour
>2 t baking powder
>1/2 t salt

1. Cream together the butter and sugar.
2. Add the egg, banana slices and milk. Beat until the mixture is smooth.
3. Add the dry ingredients and mix together.
4. Spread the batter in a greased 7" x 11" pan.

Topping

>1/3 cup brown sugar
>1/3 cup chopped walnuts, pecans or sunflower
>   kernels
>1/2 t cinnamon

5. Mix together the ingredients for the topping. Sprinkle on top of the cake and dot generously with butter.
6. Bake at 375° for 25—30 minutes.

Serves 6—9

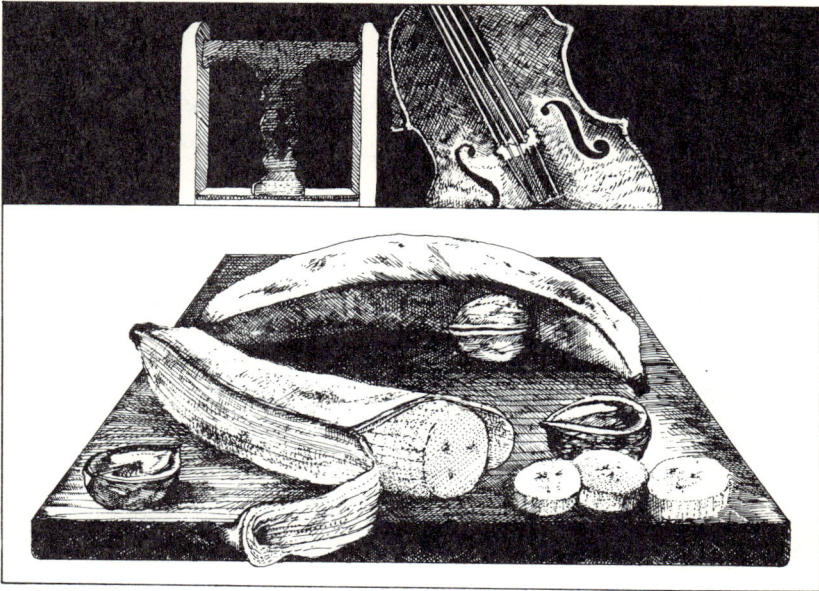

Fudge Pie

This is actually a cake, as it does not require a pie shell. It has a dense chocolate texture like fudge.

>   1/4 lb butter
>   1 cup sugar
>   2 eggs
>   1 square bitter chocolate, melted
>   1/2 cup sifted flour
>   1 t vanilla

1. Cream together the butter and sugar and beat in the eggs.
2. Add the chocolate, flour and vanilla and mix well.
3. Pour into a well greased 9″ pie plate, glass preferred.
4. Bake at 325° for 25 minutes.

Serve warm or cool in pie shaped wedges with ice cream or whipped cream or chocolate rum sauce, page 185.

Serves 6

Walnut Torte

This cake consists of a nut cake baked in layers, filled and frosted with a delicious coffee cream.

> 2 T flour
> 2 1/2 t baking powder
> 4 eggs
> 3/4 cup sugar
> 1 cup walnut halves
> toasted sliced almonds (optional)
> 1 1/2 cups heavy cream
> 1 t instant coffee, dissolved in 2 t vanilla or cognac
> 1/3 cup sugar

1. Preheat the oven to 350°. Butter generously 2 8" cake pans that are about 1 1/2" deep. Line the bottoms with waxed paper and brush the paper with additional melted butter.
2. Put the eggs and 3/4 cup sugar in the blender and whip till smooth and frothy.
3. Add the nuts and grind till fine.
4. Add the flour and baking powder and mix only until well blended.
5. Pour into the 2 pans and bake 20 minutes.
6. While the cakes are cooking, combine the 1 1/2 cups cream, coffee mixture, and sugar and beat until thick.
7. Turn the cakes out of the pans, peel off the paper, and let them cool completely. It is essential that they be well cooled before proceeding.
8. Spread the whipped coffee cream between the layers and on top, using a spatula. If desired, sprinkle the toasted almonds over the top.

Serve this cake in small wedges, as it is very rich.

Serves 6—8

Italian Rum Cake (2 Versions)

I think if Moog had to choose, this would be his absolute favorite.

Toward the end of his stay in graduate school when his assistantship ran out, he decided to go into business for himself. I looked on the decision as the kiss of death for his thesis, thinking that it would be too difficult to run a new business and work on a thesis at the same time.

So I tried a bit of feminine bribery. I told him that when he was finished writing his thesis, I'd make the biggest rum cake the world had ever seen. I can't say he wrote the thesis in a day, but within a year it was done. And I had to come through on my promise.

It dawned on me that I didn't have a huge pan to bake the cake in, so I settled for two cakes. When the cakes were ready, he cut the first one and politely served me a small portion. Then he proceeded to demolish the rest of it in one sitting. Miraculously, he didn't get a bellyache.

The next day we had four guests from the school of music whom Moog brought home for cake and coffee. He cut the second cake into six gigantic pieces, intending to share the treat with his friends. He was amazed when everyone begged off on the grounds that the servings were too big and the cake too rich. When everyone left, he finished every remaining crumb, "tst"-ing with pleasure all the while.

I hope you will like the cake as well as he did. But please remember to serve modest pieces.

Zabaglione Filled

This cake is made up of rum soaked layers filled with Zabaglione, and frosted with rum flavored whipped cream.

> 1 sponge cake recipe, baked in 3 layers
> 1 cup rum
> 1 Zabaglione recipe, page 180
> 2 cups heavy cream
> 1 T sugar
> 2–4 T rum

1. Cool the sponge cake layers while you make the Zabaglione.
2. Place the bottom layer on a serving plate and pour 1/3 cup rum over it very slowly, allowing time for the rum to soak into the cake. Spread generously with 1/2 the Zabaglione.
3. Repeat with the second layer.
4. Place the top layer on the cake and prick with a toothpick to make holes for the rum to soak into.
5. Whip the cream, adding sugar and rum. Spread on the top and sides of the cake.

Chill for 3–4 hours before serving.
This cake keeps well in the refrigerator. If you need to freeze it, place the cake uncovered in the freezer until the whipped cream is hard. Then enclose it in a plastic bag and seal tightly. The frozen cake should stand at room temperature about 10 minutes before cutting

Serves 10–12

Custard & Marmalade Filled

A couple of years ago while traveling in Ancona, Italy, Moog was invited to the home of an accordion manufacturer for dinner. The lady of the house made a rum cake that impressed Moog so much I decided to give it a try.

The cake starts with the same sponge layers as the preceding recipe, but they are soaked with sweet vermouth and filled with orange marmalade and vanilla custard. Rum is poured over all. The frosting has the same vanilla custard plus chocolate. Kiss your calorie chart goodbye!

1 sponge cake recipe
7 egg yolks
1 qt. milk
8 T sugar
8 T flour
a pinch salt
1 grated lemon rind
2 oz. unsweetened baking chocolate
12 T sweet vermouth
6 T orange marmalade
12 T sweet rum

1. Beat the egg yolks thoroughly.
2. Blend together the milk, egg yolks, sugar, flour and salt in a saucepan. Add the grated lemon rind and cook over a low flame for about 10 minutes, or until thick and barely starting to boil. Do not boil. Remove from heat.
3. Set aside 1/3 of this custard and add the chocolate to the remaining custard while it is still warm. Stir until completely melted. (If you prefer, you may add the chocolate to all the custard, so that the filling will also have chocolate in it.)
4. Place the bottom layer of the cooled sponge cake on a serving plate and pour 6 tablespoons of vermouth over it. Spread with a thin layer of marmalade and then a layer of custard. Repeat the procedure for the second layer.
5. Place the top layer on the cake. Make fine holes in it with a toothpick and pour the rum over this layer.
6. Cover the top and sides evenly with a thick layer of chocolate custard.

Refrigerate for 2—4 hours before serving.

Serves 10—12

Tosca Cake

George Kelischek and his family live in Brasstown, North Carolina, surrounded by mountains and hardwood forest. In these beautiful surroundings, he makes handmade violins, lutes, dulcimers, hurdy-gurdys and almost any other wooden instrument you can think of. He also runs a workshop called "Brasstown For Awhile" that allows individuals or whole classes to make instruments under his guidance for a modest fee. It is a unique experience in a stunning setting and, as far as I'm concerned, a bargain at twice the price.

Moog met George repeatedly at different conventions sponsored by musical instrument manufacturers. The two men liked each other and George proposed that we come down for two weeks to visit so that Moog could teach a group of young people how to make a simple electronic musical instrument. We accepted the invitation and spent two soul-satisfying weeks with the whole, warm Kelischek family.

The Kelischeks put us up and fed us dinner every evening. I offered to help by taking over dinner preparations occasionally in order to make life easier for Rosemarie Kelischek. She finally agreed to let me become the dessert chef.

By far the most favored dessert I prepared was Tosca Cake. This is so easy to make I mix it by hand. It has a light buttery texture, with a crisp almond top. Since it freezes very well, I make two or three at a time.

Cake

>   2 eggs
>   1 cup sugar
>   1 cup flour
>   2 t baking powder
>   1/2 cup milk
>   1/8 lb melted butter

1. Mix together the eggs and sugar.
2. Combine the flour, baking powder and milk and add to the eggs and sugar.
3. Mix in the melted butter.

4. Pour into an 8" x 8" greased pan and bake at 350° for 25—30 minutes. While the cake is baking, prepare the topping.

Topping

> 1/8 lb butter
> 1/4 cup sugar
> 1/2 cup slivered almonds
> 1 T flour
> 1 T milk

5. Combine the butter, sugar and almonds and heat over low heat.
6. Add the flour and milk and stir.
7. Spread this mixture over the baked cake and toast under the broiler for a few seconds until it is golden brown. This happens very fast, so keep your eye on it.

Serves 6—9

Marble Turban Cake

This is a marble pound cake baked in a turban mold, very handsome and easy to cut. It's good frosted with your favorite chocolate icing or plain with confectioners' sugar sifted over the top.

> 1/3 cup semi-sweet chocolate pieces
> 2/3 cups butter
> 1 cup sugar
> 4 eggs
> 1 3/4 cups sifted flour
> 3 t baking powder
> 1 t salt
> 1/2 cup milk
> 1 t vanilla extract

1. Melt the chocolate in a double boiler over hot water.
2. Cream the butter and sugar together thoroughly.
3. Add the eggs one at a time, beating after each addition.
4. Sift together the dry ingredients and combine the milk and vanilla extract in a separate bowl.
5. Add the dry ingredients alternately with the milk and vanilla mixture, beginning and ending with the dry ingredients. Beat smooth after each addition.
6. Put 1/3 of the batter in a separate bowl and mix with the melted chocolate.
7. Grease and flour a bundt or tube pan. Starting and ending with the white batter, alternate putting the batters into the pan so that you make 5 different layers.
8. With a knife, cut a zig-zag pattern through the batters.
9. Bake at 350° for 35—40 minutes. Let the cake cool in the pan for 15 minutes before removing it to a cooling rack.

Serves 16

TURBAN MOLD

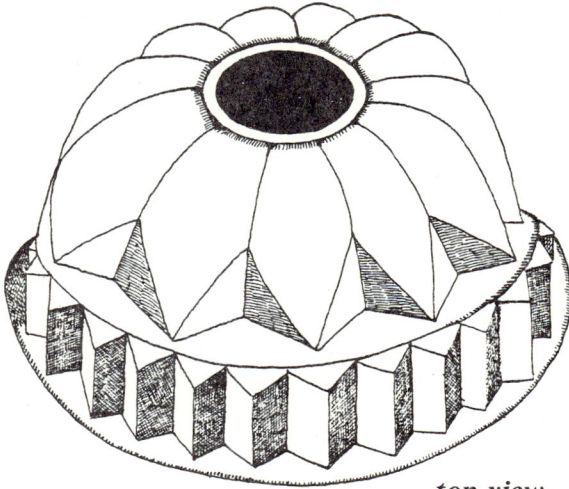

top view

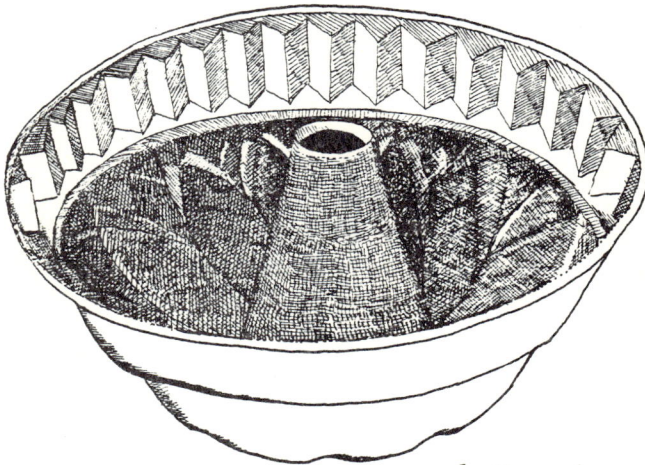

bottom view

Strawberry Nut Torte

I think this is a more toothsome answer to the strawberry season than the usual shortcake. Feather light, nut meringue layers are filled with a special whipped cream—strawberry mix and beautifully topped by glistening glazed strawberries.

Torte Layers

> 7 eggs, separated
> 1 cup sugar
> 1 cup walnuts or pecans
> 1/8 t salt
> 2 T flour

Cream Filling

> 1 pint strawberries, sliced
> 2 T sugar
> 2 T orange flavored liqueur
> 1 t gelatin
> 2 T water
> 1 cup heavy cream

Glaze

> 12 oz currant jelly
> 2 T orange flavored liqueur

Garnish

> 1 pint strawberries
> 1 cup heavy cream, whipped

1. Preheat oven to 350°.
2. To make the layers, beat the egg yolks until they are light colored and very thick. Add the sugar, a tablespoon at a time, while beating vigorously until the mixture is very thick. When the beaters are raised from the mixture, it should drop to form a rope on the surface of the batter.

3. Finely grate the walnuts or pecans. There should be 1 1/2 cups of nuts after grating. If you use a blender, do the nuts in two or three batches to keep your nut meal light.

4. Combine the nuts, salt and flour. Fold into the egg yolk mixture. Beat the egg whites until stiff, but not dry.

5. Stir 1/3 of the whites into yolk mixture. Fold in the remaining whites and turn into 2 9" layer pans which have been greased and lined on the bottom with greased wax paper.

6. Bake 35—40 minutes or until done. Set cake pans on a rack and slide a spatula around the sides of the cake to loosen. Cool in the pans 10 minutes. The layers will shrink. Remove from pans and take off wax paper. Finish cooling on the rack. Assemble cake when it is completely cool.

7. To make the filling, sprinkle sliced strawberries with liqueur and sugar. Set aside.

8. Soak the gelatin in the water and heat gently to dissolve. Beat the heavy cream and when it starts to thicken, pour in the hot gelatin mixture in a steady stream while still continuing to beat.

9. When cream mixture is very thick, fold in the strawberry mix. Use this filling between the cake layers.

10. To make the glaze, heat the currant jelly until it melts. Strain through a tea strainer and add liqueur.

11. Brush the jelly glaze over the top of the cake. Arrange the berries on top; spoon remaining glaze over the berries so they will glisten.

12. Spread the whipped cream around the outside edge of the cake. Refrigerate the cake several hours before serving.

Serves 8—10

Mini Chip Cake

This is a fine yellow cake full of small chocolate chips.

>1 cup butter
>2 cups sugar
>1 1/2 t vanilla
>3 eggs
>2 cups semi-sweet mini chocolate chips
>3 cups all-purpose flour
>2 t baking powder
>1/4 t salt
>1 cup milk
>confectioners' sugar

1. Combine the butter, sugar and vanilla in a large bowl and cream until light and fluffy.
2. Add the eggs one at a time, beating well.
3. Combine flour, baking powder and salt and add to the above mixture, alternately with the milk. Beat just until smooth.
4. Stir in the mini chips.
5. Pour into a well greased and floured 12 cup bundt pan or a 10" tube pan.
6. Bake at 350° for 1 to 1 1/4 hours.
7. Cool the cake and remove it from the pan. Sift confectioners' sugar over it just before serving.

Serves 10—12

Sour Cream Chocolate Cake

The combined flavors of sour cream and chocolate make this cake special. Our neighbor's child, who doesn't like chocolate cake, likes *this* one.

1/2 cup butter
3 oz unsweetened baking chocolate
1 cup boiling water or coffee
1 3/4 cups light brown sugar, packed down
2 cups all-purpose flour
1 1/2 t baking soda
1 t salt
2 eggs
1/2 cup sour cream
1 t vanilla

1. Combine the chocolate, butter and boiling water or coffee in a small bowl. (Coffee will give the cake a mocha-like taste.) Stir until the chocolate and butter are melted.
2. Thoroughly mix together the brown sugar, flour, baking soda and salt in a large mixing bowl.
3. Gradually add the chocolate mixture, beating until completely combined.
4. Blend in the eggs, sour cream and vanilla and beat one minute at medium speed.
5. Pour into a greased and floured 9" x 13" x 2" pan. Bake at 350° for 35—40 minutes.

Serves 8—12

Fresh Apple Cake

This is a moist spice cake liberally laced with finely chopped apples.

>   1/2 cup butter
>   1 cup sugar
>   2 eggs
>   1 1/2 cups sifted flour
>   1 t baking soda
>   3/4 t salt
>   1 t cinnamon
>   3/4 t ground cloves
>   1/2 cup cold coffee
>   2 cups raw apples, peeled and chopped
>   1 cup raisins
>   1/2 cup chopped nuts

1. Cream together the butter and sugar and then beat in the 2 eggs.
2. Mix together the flour, baking soda, salt, cinnamon and cloves.
3. Alternate adding small quantities of the flour mixture and the cold coffee to the mixture from step 1 until the ingredients are combined.
4. Stir in the apples, raisins and nuts.
5. Grease a 6 cup tube pan and fill with the cake mix.
6. Bake at 350° for about 1 hour.

CREAM CHEESE FROSTING

I like this cake plain, but if you want a frosting, this is a good one.

- 3 oz of softened cream cheese
- 1 T soft butter
- 1 t vanilla
- 2 cups sifted confectioners sugar

1. Combine the cheese, butter and vanilla in a small bowl and mix at low speed until smooth and fluffy.
2. Gradually add the confectioners sugar, beating at medium speed until smooth. The frosting is ready to be spread on the cake.

Serves 6–8

Peaches & Cream Cheesecake

This is a cheese and fruit pie that is easy to make and eat. When fresh fruits are available, you may prefer to omit the canned fruit this recipe calls for and use the glaze for Strawberry Nut Torte or cheesecake. Spoon it on *top* of the cheesecake.

 3/4 cup flour
 1 t baking powder
 1/4 t salt
 3 1/4 oz box of regular vanilla pudding
 3 T butter
 1 egg
 1/2 cup milk
 1 can sliced peaches, juice drained and reserved
 8 oz softened cream cheese
 1/2 cup sugar
 1 T sugar
 1/2 t cinnamon

1. Grease the bottom and sides of a 9" pie plate (deep), or a 10" pie plate.
2. Combine the flour, baking powder, salt, vanilla pudding, butter, egg and milk in a bowl and beat for 2 minutes at medium speed. Pour the mixture into the pie plate.
3. Arrange the fruit over the batter.
4. Combine the cream cheese, 1/2 cup sugar, and 3 tablespoons of the fruit juice in a bowl and beat 2 minutes. Spoon over the fruit in the pie plate, but leave a 1" border all around the pie.
5. Combine the 1 tablespoon sugar and the cinnamon and sprinkle over the pie.
6. Bake in a 350° oven for 30—35 minutes.

Pineapple tidbits can be used in place of the peaches.

Serves 6—8

Sister Mildred's Cream Cheese Coffee Cake

This cake reminds me of the sort of thing you take home from a favorite bakery for Sunday brunch. The recipe was my sister's treasure, but she let me have it.

1/2 - 3/4 cup chopped nuts
1 cup butter
8 oz. cream cheese
1 1/2 cup sugar
1 1/2 t vanilla
4 eggs
2 1/4 cups flour
1 1/2 t baking powder
3/4 cup currants or raisins
1/2 cup sugar
1 1/2 T cocoa
1 t cinnamon

1. Grease the bottom and sides of a 10" bundt type pan and sprinkle the nuts in the bottom of the pan.
2. Cream together the butter, cheese, 1 1/2 cups sugar and vanilla till light.
3. Add eggs to the above one at a time and beat well.
4. Gradually add the flour and baking powder, continuing to beat.
5. Fold in the currants or raisins.
6. Mix together 1/2 cup sugar, cocoa and cinnamon in a separate bowl.
7. Spoon 1/2 the batter into pan and sprinkle half of the mixture from step 6 over it. Spoon about 2/3 of the remaining batter over it and sprinkle with about 2/3 of the remaining cocoa mix. Top with the remaining batter, and swirl in the remaining cocoa mix.
8. Bake at 350° for 65—75 minutes.
9. Cool in the pan for about 15 minutes, or until the top springs back when touched, before removing from pan and serving.

Serves 8—10

Royal Pound Cake

This is a rich cake with a wonderful fragrance. Frosted or plain, this is a great basic cake.

>1 cup butter
>1 cup sugar
>4 large eggs
>juice and rind of 1 lemon
>1/2 t baking powder
>1/2 t salt
>2 cups cake flour

1. Beat together the butter and sugar till completely blended.
2. Add the eggs, one at a time, followed by lemon juice and rind, baking powder and salt.
3. Sift the flour 3 times, and then add it. Beat thoroughly.
4. Bake in a loaf pan lined with greased brown paper for 1 hour at 325°.
5. Cool the cake and remove the paper.

Mocha Frosting

>2—4 oz pkg German chocolate
>1/4 cup strong coffee
>2 T cognac
>1 1/2 cup heavy cream

1. Cut cake in 3 pieces lengthwise
2. In pan, over low heat, melt chocolate in coffee. Mix until smooth.
3. Stir in cognac and cool in refrigerator.
4. Whip cream and fold in cooled mocha mixture.
5. Spread each layer with filling and frost top.
6. Chill several hours.

Serves 6

Poor Man's Cake

This is a good spice cake that costs next to nothing to make.

  1 cup sugar
  1 cup raisins
  1/2 cup lard
  1 cup cold water
  1/2 t nutmeg
  1/2 t cinnamon
  1 t salt
  1 1/2 cups flour
  1 t baking soda dissolved in 2 T cold water

1. Combine the first 7 ingredients in a saucepan and bring to a boil. Cool.
2. Mix together the flour and baking soda mixture and add to the above mixture after it has cooled. Mix well.
3. Bake in a greased 8" x 8" pan at 350° for 1 hour.

Serve warm or cool with vanilla sauce.

Vanilla Sauce

  1/2 cup sugar
  1 t vanilla
  1 T cornstarch
  2 T butter
  1 cup boiling water
  a pinch of salt

1. Mix together sugar, cornstarch and salt. Add to the boiling water and cook until it has thickened.
2. Add the vanilla and butter and mix till the sauce is smooth.

If you're not feeling too poor, add a couple of tablespoons of heavy cream to make a richer sauce.

Serves 6—9

Baklava

This is a rich, layered pastry composed of buttered filo leaves, ground nuts and spices, gently bathed with a warm honey-lemon-spice bath. It is very rich, but superb in small pieces. You can buy filo leaves at Greek grocery stores.

Filling

> 3 cups ground nuts (walnuts, almonds or pecans
> > or a mixture)
>
> 1/3 cup sugar
> 1/2 t cinnamon
> 1/8 t cloves
> 1 lb filo pastry
> 1 1/2 cup sweet butter, melted

Syrup

> 1 3/4 cup water
> 3/4 cup brown sugar
> 3/4 cup honey
> 3 whole cloves, plus a pinch of powdered cloves
> 1/2 lemon–juice, pulp and finely sliced peel

1. In small bowl, mix ground nuts, sugar, and spices, for filling.
2. Place 2 leaves of filo pastry in a 10" x 15" x 1" buttered jellyroll pan and brush generously with melted butter.
3. Repeat above procedure using 10 leaves in all and buttering every other leaf. Cover the unused filo leaves with plastic so they don't dry out.
4. Sprinkle the filo leaves with 1/4 of the nut mixture and then add 6 more leaves buttering every other leaf and sprinkling with 1/4 of the original nut mixture.
5. Repeat above 3 times, ending with 10 leaves for the top layer, buttering as above.
6. Bake for 45 minutes in a 350° oven. Turn off heat and leave baklava in oven for 45 minutes longer.

7. Make syrup by combining all syrup ingredients in saucepan and bringing to a boil, stirring until sugar is dissolved.
8. Reduce heat and simmer syrup uncovered 15—20 minutes.
9. Strain syrup.
10. When baklava is removed from the oven, pour the syrup over the top.
11. Cool in pan on wire rack for 1 1/2—2 hours.
12. Cut into diamond shaped pieces and let pastry stand in pan, *lightly* covered with Saran wrap, overnight.

Makes about 32 pieces

Greatgrandma's Spongecake

This is a fine textured, light sponge cake that is a snap to make. Its originator is Moog's paternal grandmother, our children's great-grandma. It's the best sponge cake I ever tasted.

yolks of 5 eggs
2 cups sugar
a pinch salt
juice and grated rind of 1 orange

1/2 cup water
2 1/4 cups flour
2 t baking powder
whites of 4 eggs

1. Cream together the egg yolks and sugar, and add the salt and orange rind.
2. Stir in the water.
3. Sift in the flour and baking powder, and beat thoroughly.
4. Add the orange juice.
5. Beat the egg whites until stiff, and gently fold into the cake batter.
6. Bake in a greased and floured tube pan for 1 hour at 350°.

Serves 6—8

Cookies & Bars

Date Nut Bars

These bars are flavored with brown sugar, dates and nuts. They are chewy, fine with a fruit dessert.

> 1 1/2 cup sifted flour
> 1 t baking powder
> 1 t salt
> 2 cups brown sugar
> 1/2 cup butter, melted
> 4 eggs
> 2 cups chopped nuts
> 2 cups chopped dates

1. Sift flour, baking powder and salt.
2. Combine above with brown sugar.
3. Add melted butter to 4 beaten eggs and mix with dry ingredients.
4. Add nuts and dates and mix well.
5. Bake in 2 greased 9" x 9" x 1" pans in 350° oven for 25 minutes.
6. Let cool and cut into bars.

These freeze well.

Makes about 50 bars

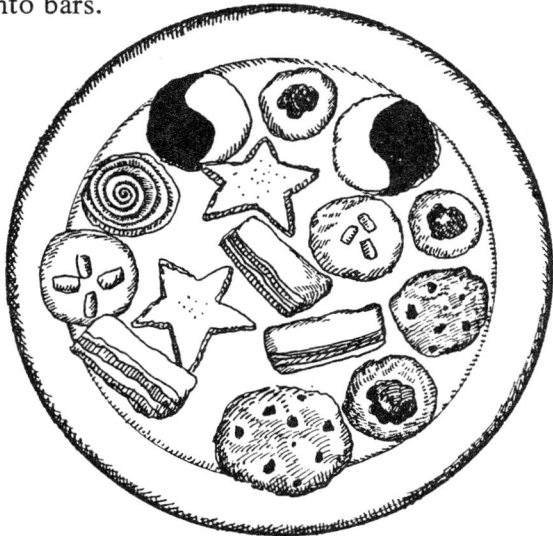

English Toffee Bars

The toffee flavor and the thick shell of semi-sweet chocolate make these bars a bit unusual—nice to have tucked away in the freezer.

    1 cup brown sugar
    1/4 cup butter
    1 egg
    1/4 t salt
    3/4 cup flour
    1/2 t baking powder
    1 t vanilla
    1 cup semi-sweet bits
    1/2 cup toasted, chopped almonds

1. Combine sugar, butter, egg, salt, flour, baking powder and vanilla in mixer and beat until well blended.
2. Butter an 8" x 8" pan, pour in the batter and bake at 350° for 20 minutes.
3. Cool in pan and spread with 1 cup melted semi-sweet chocolate bits.
4. Sprinkle with 1/2 cup of toasted chopped almonds.
5. Allow chocolate to harden. Cut in bars 1" x 2".

Makes 32

Lace Wafers

These delicate, tube shaped wafers are a web-like filigree of almonds and butter. They are good anytime but I especially like them with tea, fruit or fruited desserts.

    1/2 cup sweet butter
    1/2 cup sugar
    3 T flour
    a pinch of nutmeg
    2 T milk
    1/8 t salt
    1/2 cup finely chopped toasted and skinless
            almonds

1. In a saucepan over medium heat cook and stir in the butter, sugar, flour, nutmeg, milk, salt and nuts until smooth.
2. Drop the batter by level tablespoonful onto a lightly greased and floured cookie sheet, 4″ apart. Don't crowd the cookies. Remember to grease and flour the cookie sheet for each batch.
3. Bake at 350° for 6−8 minutes, or till lightly browned.
4. Let them cool slightly on the baking sheet, then lift them off with a wide spatula and wrap around a broomstick handle to shape. Cool.

These cookies must be stored in an air-tight metal container, or they will lose their crispness.

Makes about 18 cookies

Graham Bars

One evening, the wife of one of our technicians showed up at the farm house door with a plate of cookies. By the time the plate was half empty, everyone agreed it was a recipe I should have.

These are sweet, chocolaty bars, loved by men, children, and ladies who don't have to give their figure a second thought— as I said, men and children.

> 2 cups graham cracker crumbs (about 24 crackers)
> 1 can condensed milk
> 1/2 cup finely chopped walnuts or pecans
> 1 pkg semi-sweet chocolate bits
> 1 t vanilla
> granulated sugar
> 1/2 t cinnamon

1. Grease 8″ x 8″ pan.
2. Blend crumbs, condensed milk, nuts, chocolate pieces, cinnamon and vanilla.
3. Pour mixture into greased pan, spreading evenly.
4. Bake in 350° oven about 30 minutes.
5. Cool in pan on cake rack 5 minutes. Loosen around edges with sharp knife, cut into bars, remove from pan and sprinkle with granulated sugar.

Makes 16 bars

Puddings, Custards & Souffles
Zabaglione

This delicate custard gets its distinctive taste from Marsala, a heavy, sweet Italian sherry. It's best served with a dollop of real whipped cream on top. It refrigerates very well.

An interesting diet note—this dessert is permissible on a low carbohydrate diet. One portion contains only a small amount of sugar and sherry. Eggs and whipped cream have no carbohydrate value.

> **6 egg yolks**
> **6 half eggshells full of Marsala wine**
> **6 teaspoons sugar**

1. Break yolks in top of double boiler. Add sugar and beat with egg beater until light lemon colored and thoroughly blended.
2. Add Marsala. Sometimes instead of Marsala, I use cognac for a sharper taste. 1—2 half eggshells full of cognac is sufficient.
3. Place boiling water in lower part of double boiler. Cook egg mixture over boiling water about 5 minutes or until it begins to thicken. Be sure to beat constantly while the mixture is cooking. Do not allow to boil.
4. Remove from fire immediately at first sign of a bubble. Pour into parfait glasses. Cool and serve.

Serves 6

Caramel Custard

Nona Trythall, a beautiful, small-boned, raven haired young woman, specializes in prints made by etching lead. She and her husband, Richard, lived in Buffalo for a while until the siren call of Rome became too loud to withstand.

My caramel custard or "flan" was dessert one night and Nona pronounced it "super."

It is a classic Spanish dessert which may be made in individual portions or in a large bundt pan or souffle dish for a more gala appearance. Its taste is rich and gentle. The caramel makes a butterscotch colored top, with a plentiful sauce.

> 1 cup sugar
> 5 eggs
> 1 1/2 t vanilla
> pinch of salt
> 2 cups milk
> 2 cups evaporated milk
> 1 cup sugar

1. In an iron skillet, melt a cup of sugar stirring constantly; it will be medium brown in color. (To clean the skillet, fill it with hot water and boil. It will rinse out immediately.)
2. Cover the bottom of flan container with melted sugar. It will harden almost immediately.
3. Beat together eggs, vanilla and salt.
4. Heat evaporated and regular milk to scalding with one cup of sugar. (Scalding means the milk bubbles around the edge of the pot but does not boil.)
5. Add to egg mixture beating constantly.
6. Fill caramel lined dish 3/4 full of flan mixture.
7. Place in pan filled with an inch or so of hot water and bake at 400° for 40—50 minutes or until custard is set.
8. Cool. Refrigerate overnight and invert to serve. Use a large plate as the caramel makes its own sauce. If there is too much for your liking, you may serve it in a separate small pitcher.

I prefer the bundt pan for this custard because of its decorative molding and also because the design makes cutting easy.

Serves 12

Apricot Souffle

If you can afford the apricots, this frozen dessert is easy to make and goes a long way. Besides that, it is de luxe.

> 1 box (11 oz) dried apricots
> water
> 1 1/4 cups sugar (3/4 cup white and 1/2 cup brown)
> 4 eggs, separated
> 2 cups heavy cream

1. Cover apricots with water in a saucepan. Bring to boil and simmer 15 minutes. Drain, reserving 1/2 cup of liquid.
2. Puree apricots in blender or force through food mill.
3. Blend 1 cup of sugar (1/2 cup brown, 1/2 cup white) and reserved liquid in saucepan; add egg yolks and beat until blended. Cook, stirring constantly until mixture is thick enough to coat a metal spoon. Combine with apricot puree in large bowl and let cool.
4. Meanwhile, cut a 4″ strip of foil or waxed paper long enough to wrap around the outside of a round, straight sided souffle dish or casserole which measures 4 cups to the brim. Tape or rubber-band collar on the outside of dish so collar stands 2″ above rim.
5. Beat egg whites until stiff peaks form. Gradually, add remaining sugar (1/4 cup white) beating until stiff peaks form. Fold into the apricot mixture. Whip cream with clean beater and fold in. Pour mixture into prepared souffle dish. Freeze overnight or at least 5 hours. Souffle may be enclosed in a plastic bag and frozen for 1 month.
6. When ready to serve, remove collar and let stand 20 minutes at room temperature. Serve modest portions. This is a *rich* dessert.

Serves 10–12

Coffee Custard

This custard makes a lovely end to a heavy meal or a treat for breakfast.

   3 eggs
   1/3 cup sugar
   1/2 t salt
   2 T instant coffee
   1 t vanilla
   2 1/4 cups milk

1. Preheat the oven to 375°.
2. Beat the eggs slightly and stir in the sugar, salt, instant coffee and vanilla extract.
3. Heat the milk until a film forms on the surface.
4. Very gradually beat the milk into the egg mixture.
5. Pour into a medium size souffle dish.
6. Place the dish in a pan filled with 2" of water, and bake for 30 minutes or until a toothpick inserted in the center comes out clean.

   You can make this custard another way. Fit a large Dutch oven with an improvised rack. (A round cookie rack is fine.) Fill with 2 or 3" of water and bring to a boil. Place the souffle dish, covered with foil, on the rack and cover the Dutch oven. Simmer over low heat 45 minutes or an hour. This method gives a more coarse texture, which I like. When you are using a wood cookstove, this method works well.
7. Chill and serve cold, either plain or with whipped cream and a dash of nutmeg.

Serves 6–8

Bread Pudding

This is not, strictly speaking, a dessert. It may be eaten at any meal plain or with fruit and/or sausages, much like pancakes.

> 3 cups dark or light bread, or stale cake (an
>   assortment will make it interesting)
> 3 cups milk
> 1 T brown sugar
> 1 T white sugar
> 1 T honey or molasses
> 3 eggs
> 1 or 2 cups dates, raisins and nuts
> 1 or 2 T apricot jelly
> 1/2 cup applesauce or diced fresh apple
> 1/8 lb melted butter
> 1 banana
> 1 drop vanilla
> 1/4 t baking soda
> 1 tiny glass red wine
> 1 t cinnamon
> 1/2 t nutmeg

1. Soak the bread pieces in the warm milk.
2. Add all the other ingredients except the eggs.
3. Separate the eggs. Mix the egg yolks into the bread mixture.
4. Beat the egg whites until stiff and gently fold them into the bread mix.
5. Grease a large pan and spread the mixture out on it. Bake 45–60 minutes at 350°, or until golden brown and firm.

This pudding is good served with heavy cream as a topping.

If you want, you can vary this recipe to make nifty hamburger shaped pancakes. Leave out a little of the wet ingredients, shape the mixture into thick pancakes and fry them in butter. Serve with honey, maple syrup, or preserves.

Serves 10–12

Ice Cream, Toppings & Candy
Mocha Rum Sauce

This sauce is super if you're a hot fudge nut. Unlike other recipes I've tried, this sauce remains liquid when poured over ice cream. It also dresses up a piece of pound cake.

8 oz semi-sweet chocolate bits
1/4 cup sugar
1/2 cup strong black coffee (instant is all right)
1 T butter
2 T rum (or cognac)
1/4 t vanilla

1. Melt the chocolate in the top of a double boiler over hot water on medium heat.
2. Add the sugar, coffee and butter, one at a time, and mix well.
3. Cook for 10 minutes over medium heat.
4. Remove from heat and stir in the liquor and vanilla.

Makes about 1 1/2 cups

Butterscotch Sauce

This is an old family recipe belonging to our friend and neighbor, Ann Moore. It is soooo easy to make—turns vanilla ice cream into a super treat.

2 cups brown sugar
1/2 pint heavy cream
1/2 lb butter
nuts to sprinkle over the top (optional)

1. Put all the ingredients except the nuts in the top of a double boiler. Fill the bottom with enough water to barely touch the bottom of the top pot. Bring the water to a boil.
2. Simmer slowly for 1 hour, stirring now and then. Serve warm. Good with toasted walnuts or filberts sprinkled on top.

Makes enough for 12—18

Brandied Fruit

Fresh fruit, brandy and sugar combine to make an ambrosia-like sauce to serve over ice cream or angel food cake. It's also good served by itself with a bit of whipped cream as a topping. The juice is like a fruit brandy, lovely served at room temperature or with ice, club soda and a twist of lemon.

Ein Kleine Kitchen Music—When I was first married, I was thumbing through a cookbook and found this recipe which sounded wonderful. Alas, we lived in an attic apartment which had no place cool enough for me to store the fruit. Many years later we were renting a large country house which had a basement. There was only one hitch: we were scheduled to move in midsummer. I decided I'd start the crock going in the house and pray that we'd find an apartment where I could continue to store it.

My anticipation was high after so many years of waiting. I started a double batch. Moog passed many fruit stands on his way to and from Cornell and brought home many quarts of fine fruit. When we moved to a new apartment, I explained the problem to my landlady, asking her if I could have one tiny spot in her basement. She agreed.

When we moved to the apartment, I kept the crock in the kitchen adding fruit to it throughout the fruit season. In September, I asked for my cool spot only to be told by the landlady that she had changed her mind; she didn't want strangers in her basement. What to do? I had a cabinet on the floor which wasn't close to a heat register. It qualified as the coolest spot in the apartment. Moog made me a wooden top for the crock and I stored it there.

In October we had to go to New York for an Audio Engineering Society Show. It was unseasonably warm, Indian summer and we had a fine time. The Synthesizer got a good, if puzzled, reception from the audio world. After I arrived home, I took a peek at my brew. Tens of thousands of fruit flies were lining the sides of the crock and surface of the brew. Because the weather was warm and the cover not air tight, we had a catastrophe. I was sick about the whole scene.

Since then I am very cautious. I make any addition of fruit to the crock that I want, leave it out a few days tightly covered and then refrigerate it until I make another addition. When the process is finished, I keep it in the refrigerator unless I get short of room. In that case, I keep it next to a cold window until the refrigerator load lightens. Forewarned is forearmed.

To make brandied fruit, you cannot use apples (the skins are too hard), bananas (too soft) or grapes, gooseberries and other fruits (the skins get tough).

1. Place in a stone crock with a tight fitting lid (or a jar begged from a deli)

> **1 qt brandy (the better the brandy, the better**
> **the fruit)**
> **2 cups sugar**

2. Add, as they come into season, a quart of each

> **strawberries**
> **cherries (pitted)**
> **raspberries**
> **peaches, peeled and sliced**
> **pineapple chunks**

With the addition of each quart of fruit, add 2 cups of sugar. Keep tasting, and if it gets too sweet for your taste, skip the sugar with the next fruit addition.
3. Stir the fruit every day until the last fruit has been added. The soft berries will dissolve to make a fruity liqueur base.
4. Cover the crock well and keep in the refrigerator or a very cool place.

It will keep for at least a year.

Yield about 1 gallon

Marron Glace

A few years after Moog started his business and we were more relaxed about money, Moog read an article about a restaurant in New York with a famous chef. Since one of Moog's desires is to be a chef, he suggested on our next trip to the city we eat there. The restaurant was incredibly expensive, but we thought the meal and ambience justified the price. However, the dessert, though delicious, was outrageously priced. It was—a small scoop of vanilla ice cream, two candied chestnuts (Marron Glace) and a bit of glace sauce. Price—$5.00 for two sundaes.

I vowed to find the recipe. It took a bit of hunting, but I found it. Now when I see chestnuts, I buy a lb and make a quart. They will keep about a month in the refrigerator, but usually don't last that long, at least in our household.

> 1 lb chestnuts
> 1 cup sugar
> 1 cup water
> dash salt
> 1/4 t lemon juice
> 1/2 t vanilla

1. Make an "X" with a sharp knife in the flat part of each chestnut and roast in a 350° oven on a broiling tray until the "X" spreads open.
2. Remove the shell and fuzzy skin, trying to keep the chestnut whole. However, if it breaks, it is not a tragedy.
3. Make a syrup of sugar, water and salt and cook over low heat for about 10 minutes.
4. Simmer chestnuts in syrup for about 30–45 minutes until they begin to look translucent.
5. Add lemon juice and vanilla to syrup and put in quart bottle. Store in frig and use as needed. Quite a treat served plain with a bit of whipped cream.

If you are not big ice cream people, maybe you could make a gift of some of the chestnuts to another ice cream nut.

Make this sauce as soon as you buy the chestnuts. The nuts tend to dry in the shells and are not as soft as they should be to be thoroughly enjoyable.

You can use walnuts or pecans and the resulting sauce is very much like the ice cream garnish one buys in tiny bottles in the super market, but much less expensive. No baking of the nuts is required. Just shell them and put the halves in the syrup.

Makes about a quart

Nesselrode Sauce

Candied fruit, nuts and rum make this ice cream sauce very special. It is grand to store in the refrigerator to use on special occasions or to give away for presents.

   1 1/2 cups sugar
   2 cups water
   1/2 cup white corn syrup
   1/2 cup each of candied orange and lemon peel
   1 cup candied cherries
   1/4 cup mixed candied fruits
   1 cup slivered almonds, or your favorite nuts
   3/4 cup light or dark rum

1. Cook the first three ingredients to 240°.
2. Add the fruits and nuts and bring to a boil again. Take the pan off the heat.
3. Stir in the rum. Chill before using.

Makes 3 cups

Whipped Cream

Why anybody buys all the ersatz concoctions that come in
squirt cans is beyond me. Heavy cream is between 25–50 cents
a cup depending on the season. Converting it to whipped cream
is a cinch.

> 1 cup heavy cream
> 1 t vanilla extract
> 1 T sugar

Combine ingredients and whip with hand rotary or electric
beater until soft peaks form. That's it folks. Use it to frost
cakes, spoon on desserts, in a steaming cup of black coffee.

Honey Almond Parfait

This makes a simple but lovely dessert.

> honey
> almonds
> vanilla ice cream

In a high parfait glass, put several thin layers in this order: ice
cream, 1 to 2 teaspoons of honey, a sprinkle of almonds. End
with the almonds on top. Cut the almonds in slivers. They can
be toasted if you like or sauteed in butter and then sprinkled
with a tablespoon of sugar and a pinch of cinnamon.

Orange Ice Cream

Whenever there is a sale on heavy cream, I zip right out and scoop up an armful for desserts. The following ice creams and milks can all be made in a pan in your kitchen freezer—no salt or churning required.

    4 egg yolks
    2/3 cup sugar
    1/8 t salt
    6 oz frozen orange juice concentrate, thawed
                (don't dilute)
    2 cups half and half
    2 cups heavy cream, whipped

1. Beat the egg yolks until thick and lemon colored.
2. Gradually beat in the sugar and salt.
3. Stir in the thawed orange juice concentrate, and the half and half.
4. Fold in the whipped cream.
5. Pour into freezer trays or lasagne pan and freeze until mushy.
6. Stir and freeze until solid.

Makes 2 quarts

Variation— Orange Swirl

When the ice cream is almost frozen solid, stir in 6 oz frozen orange juice concentrate, thawed and undiluted. Stir just enough to make a marble pattern; do not mix completely.

Biscuit Tortoni

This is an easy, wickedly fattening dessert.

> 6 T confectioners' sugar
> 1 cup heavy cream
> 1 egg white
> 3 T rum
> 4 t toasted, sliced almonds

1. Whip cream.
2. Add sugar and rum. Beat until stiff.
3. Fold in beaten egg white.
4. Place 2 or 3 heaping tablespoons of mix in paper muffin cups or white pleated paper candy cups which can be purchased in a stationery store.
5. Sprinkle each with toasted almonds.
6. Freeze until ready to serve.

Makes 8 large portions

Lemon Ice Milk

The fruity acid taste of this dessert is pleasing in the summer or after a big meal.

> 1 cup half and half
> 1 cup heavy cream
> 1 cup sugar
> 1/2 T fresh grated lemon peel
> 1/3 cup fresh lemon juice and pulp

1. Stir together the half and half, heavy cream and sugar until the sugar is dissolved.
2. Mix in the lemon peel, juice and pulp.
3. Pour into ice cube trays and freeze several hours until firm.

Half and half cream may be purchased or made at home by mixing equal quantities of milk and heavy cream.

Makes about 1 1/2 pints

Molasses Ice Cream

This recipe turns out a smooth ice cream free of ice crystals. The credit goes to the molasses. When I've substituted other flavorings without the viscous qualities of molasses, the product is always crystalline.

> 1 cup milk
> 1/4 cup sugar
> dash salt
> 2 eggs, beaten
> 1/4 cup molasses
> 1 cup heavy cream, whipped

1. Scald milk. Add sugar and salt and mix.
2. Stir a small amount into slightly beaten eggs. Add to remaining milk in pan.
3. Cook in double boiler over low heat, stirring constantly until mixture coats a metal spoon.
4. Stir in molasses. Chill.
5. Fold in whipped cream. Pour into freezer tray or sheet cake pan and put in freezer. Stir and beat with a wooden spoon 2–3 times during freezing when crystals begin to form.
6. After last beating, store in plastic refrigerator container.

Serves 6–8

Brandy Balls

Wafer crumbs, brandy, rum, honey and ground walnuts combine to make these lovely treats. They improve with age.

    2 pkg (4 3/4 oz each) vanilla wafers
    1/4 cup brandy
    1/4 cup rum
    1/2 cup honey
    1 lb ground walnuts (5 1/2 cups)
    confectioners' sugar

1. Grind the vanilla wafers and mix with the other ingredients except the sugar.
2. Form into small balls and roll in sugar.
   Store in tightly covered containers.

Sour Cream Raisin Fudge

This is a creamy fudge made with yellow raisins.

    2 cups granulated sugar
    1/2 cup sour cream
    1/3 cup white corn syrup
    2 T butter
    1/4 t salt
    2 t vanilla, rum, or brandy flavoring
    1/2 cup golden raisins

1. Grease a shallow pan. A pie plate works well.
2. Combine the first 5 ingredients in a sauce pan. Bring to a boil slowly and stir until the sugar dissolves. Boil without stirring over medium heat to 236° on a candy thermometer, or until the mixture forms a soft ball when dropped in cold water.
3. Remove from heat and let stand 15 minutes. Do not stir.
4. Add flavoring and beat with a wooden spoon until the mixture starts to lose its gloss. This will take about 8 minutes.
5. Stir in the raisins and pour quickly into the greased pan.
6. Cool and cut into squares.

Fruited Desserts
Rhubarb & Heavy Cream

One summer when we were having the bottom floor of our farmhouse remodeled, I was a captive in three rooms upstairs. To spur the workmen on, I would serve coffee and cake each morning and something cold in the afternoon. One morning I harvested a great amount of rhubarb, froze some and cooked a big bowlful of the rest. I also happened to have a quart of fresh heavy cream in the house which a farmer friend had given me. That afternoon I served the workmen small dishes of ice cold rhubarb covered with cream. The workmen, all country lads who were brought up on Mom's runny rhubarb, demurred politely. I smiled and said rhubarb was all I had for them that afternoon. I left the room but didn't take the rhubarb with me. In a few minutes they were knocking at my door upstairs asking for more. Some credit for this success goes to my method of cooking rhubarb—much credit goes to the lush heavy cream I served it with.

Rhubarb is a vegetable with red stalks which requires a lot of sugar to make it palatable. It cooks up to a runny sauce if left to its own devices. My secret is tapioca which produces a thick sauce with the refreshing spring taste of rhubarb.

4 cups rhubarb stalks cut in 1″ pieces
1 cup water
1 1/2—2 cups white or brown sugar
3—4 T minute tapioca

1. Place the rhubarb pieces in a pan with the water, tapioca and 1 cup of sugar. Partially cover and cook slowly until the rhubarb begins to disintegrate. Stir occasionally to keep the rhubarb from sticking.
2. Add the remaining sugar, mix and taste. If you think it needs more sugar, go ahead and add it. Cook 5 minutes more and pour into a large bowl.

The rhubarb will thicken as it cools. Refrigerate and serve cold with heavy cream or some good cookies.

Serves 6—8

Gelatin Desserts

I am tired of the oversugared, pale flavored gelatin desserts sold in the supermarket. I've found that making your own takes only a few minutes longer than opening a boxed dessert. The results are worth the extra time.

> **2 packets gelatin (2 T)**
> **2/3 cup sugar**
> **1/4 t salt**
> **3 1/2 cups hot juice**

1. Mix the gelatin, sugar and salt together in a bowl.
2. Strain the fruit, canned or frozen and thawed. Measure the juice. Add enough water or apple juice to make 3 1/2 cups. Heat the liquid almost to the boiling point.
3. Add the hot liquid to the gelatin, sugar and salt. Stir until gelatin is dissolved.
4. Pour into a mold and chill till firm. Unmold and serve.
5. If you want to use fruit in the gelatin, add 1/2 tablespoon of gelatin to the above recipe. Chill the gelatin until the consistency of unbeaten egg whites. Add 1—2 cups of fruit and mix gently.

Serve either plain or with cream, whipped or unwhipped.

Makes 6—8 servings.

Suggested Flavors

frozen raspberries
canned crushed pineapple
grape juice and bananas
orange juice with peaches or bananas
orange juice with mandarin oranges
apple juice with canned peaches and 1/2 t nutmeg

Cherry Dumplings

These provide a solid end to a light meal. They are very easy to do—I've even made these over a campfire.

> 1 cup canned pitted sour red cherries
> 1 cup sugar
> 7/8 cup sifted unbleached flour
> 1 t baking powder
> 1/4 t salt
> grated orange rind
> 1/3 cup milk
> 2 t butter, melted

1. Put the undrained cherries and 3/4 cup sugar in a large deep skillet and bring to a boil.
2. Sift 1/4 cup sugar, flour, baking powder and salt together.
3. Add the remaining ingredients to the sugar and flour mixture of step 2, and mix lightly.
4. Drop the batter by spoonfuls into the boiling cherry mixture, making 4—6 dumplings.
5. Cover and cook gently for 20 minutes.
6. Serve warm, with whipped cream and nutmeg, if you like.

These dumplings are good served as a side dish with pork or ham.

If you have 4—6 in your family, better double the recipe. Everyone, especially the children, will want one more.

Makes 4—6 servings

Applesauce

Applesauce is a very simple year-round dessert. The best apple-sauce is always homemade, so if you have never made your own, give it a try. You'll never buy that store stuff again.

> 3 lbs apples, washed and cut into quarters
> 1/2 cup brown sugar
> sprinkle of cinnamon
> sprinkle of nutmeg
> 1 orange, quartered and the rind grated
> raisins (optional)
> nuts (optional)
> orange juice (optional)

1. Put the quartered apples into a pot with 1/2 cup water, the sugar, cinnamon, nutmeg, orange and orange rind. If your apples are very dry, add some butter and slightly more liquid.
2. Cook over low heat, mixing the top apples to the bottom often to help the cooking. If necessary, add another 1/2 cup water.
3. Cook until a soft sauce is formed, and then puree the apple-sauce.
4. While it is still hot, taste to see if more sweetening is needed. You can add more sugar, or honey.

This can be served warm or cold, as a dessert or as a side dish.

Makes 1/2 gallon

CHUNKY APPLESAUCE

This sauce is basically the same as the above one, except you must peel the apples. Cook them until soft but not mushy. Do not strain or puree.

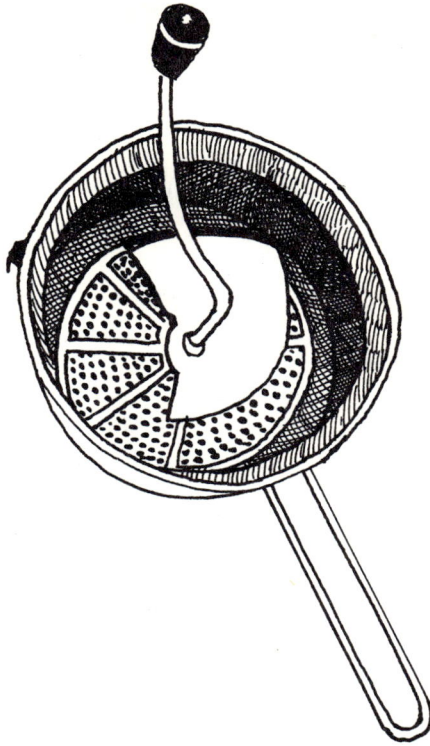

Apple Raisin Nut Crepe

Crepe recipe, page 86
12 medium apples, skinned, cored & sliced
3/4 cup raisins
1/2 cup nuts, walnuts or pecans
cinnamon
nutmeg
butter
2–3 T tapioca
1/2–1 cup sugar

1. Fill a 12" frying pan with apple slices, raisins, nuts.
2. Sprinkle to taste with cinnamon and nutmeg.
3. Sprinkle with tapioca and sugar.
4. Add a third of a cup of water. Cover and simmer until the apples are soft and the tapioca has begun to thicken the mixture.
5. Put about 1 T of the filling on each crepe cover. Fold as instructed on page
6. Place in greased pan. Put a dollop of butter on each crepe. Sprinkle all with cinnamon sugar.
7. Broil the crepes, but watch them closely. Remove the pan when the crepes are browned and puffed, and the filling is warmed.
8. Serve with whipped cream, sour cream or yogurt, whichever is your favorite.

Serves 12.

Drinks

Drinks

Coffee For 1 or 100

I have never hired one of those huge coffee makers even when we have a crowd at our house. We like pot coffee better than coffee made in any other way. We've tried all the different methods for making coffee, percolators, drip pots, automatic coffee makers—we always come back to pot coffee for its rich, full taste. Whenever I make pot coffee, people always ask me what kind of coffee maker I use and what brand of coffee. When I tell them, they are amazed.

Except for rare occasions, I buy the strongest brand of A & P coffee, unground. I grind it fresh at home in a coffee grinder. For 50—100 people, I use my big enameled canning pot. I measure 1 tablespoon of coffee for every cup of water. Then I put in an extra cupful of coffee for the pot. Sometimes I sneak in a bit of Medaglia D'Oro demitasse coffee for extra rich, robust taste. In detail, this is what I do.

1. Boil water
2. Add 1 tablespoon coffee to each cup of water and boil 5 minutes.
3. Turn off heat and let grounds settle 5 minutes.
4. If you don't mind a few grounds in your cup, ladle out the coffee. If you do mind the grounds, strain it into a serving pitcher. Serve with cream and sugar.

My everyday, family coffee pot, my only coffee pot, is an L. L. Bean spatter design, 25 cup, camping pot. It comes with a perking mechanism which is sitting unused in my house, somewhere in a closet. I treat the pot like a saucepan and make coffee in it by the above method. It has one advantage over a saucepan, a spout with a built in strainer which eliminates the coffee grounds. Beware spatter design camping pots in your hardware store which have a seam around the bottom. These leak very quickly. The L.L. Bean coffee pot is seamless on the bottom. It has performed faithfully for many years.

Brewing Tea In Small
And Large Quantities

Until recently, my favorite teas were Lapsang Souchong, green tea and a spicy concoction of my own. Lately, I've tried some of the herb teas and I like them very much, especially with honey. My children love herb teas too—it's nice to be able to brew a pot of tea in the morning and share it with the family.

Tea, like coffee, can be brewed in a large clean stainless steel pot if you are making a large quantity. It can then be decanted to a teapot or serving pitcher, preferably made of pottery. A low flame will help keep the reserved tea hot and ready to serve. I usually add a teaspoon of tea for every cup of brewed tea that I want, or 1 teabag for every 2 cups of brewed tea. Remember to remove the leaves or bags when the tea is the strength you desire or the beverage will be too potent and unpalatable. I serve lemon and honey with tea. Another addition which is very pleasant is a teaspoon of homemade jam to a hot mug of tea.

In the summer I make iced tea by the gallon in a big plastic decanter. Iced herb teas are very refreshing also. For iced tea, I make a strong tea base of 6 teabags to 6 cups of boiling water. After allowing the tea to steep for about 10 minutes, I remove the tea or bags and dilute the base with the juice of 3 lemons and fruit juice or ginger ale ice cubes and/or water until I have a gallon. I add the lemons (what's left from the juicing) and some mint leaves and chill the tea. The lemons should not remain in the tea more than one day because they get mushy. Orange juice is my preference for juice cubes.

If you are making a small quantity of tea, follow the proportions listed above. You can boil the water in a stainless steel pot. Heat up the pottery teapot by letting a cup of boiling water sit in it for a few minutes and then discard the water. Put your tea leaves or bag(s) at the bottom of the pot. Pour in the fresh hot water. The tea will be ready in 5 minutes.

Sangria a la Moog

In 1970, Moog was invited to attend a Billboard convention in Majorca to accept a Trendsetter award. He wasn't especially excited about going, since he had never been there and was convinced that it had no appeal. I couldn't go since our youngest child Matthew had just been born. Moog went reluctantly and came back with glowing reports of Mediterranean sunsets and sangria. I've been kicking myself ever since for not going with him. I'll never try for martyrdom again.

    1/2 lemon
    1/2 orange
    1/2 cup brandy
    1/4 cup Cointreau or other orange flavor liqueur
    ice cubes
    2 T powdered sugar
    1 bottle light dry red wine, preferably Rioja district
                wine
    12 oz club soda

1. Slice lemon and orange thinly and remove seeds.
2. Put in a strong 1 gallon glass pitcher. Add 1 tray of ice cubes, brandy, Cointreau and sugar.
3. Stir vigorously with a wooden spoon to bruise the fruit slices.
4. Add wine and club soda. Stir a bit.
5. Fasten seat belt and drink.

Sangria is a creeper-upper. It tastes like a lovely, long fruity drink and you tend to drink a lot of it. Then, pow! Don't say I didn't warn you.

Wine Punch

This wine punch has served me well for many years. It is classy and not too expensive, most refreshing on a warm evening. The brandied peaches and strawberries look nice and taste terrific. All the ingredients except the peaches should be chilled.

    1/2 gallon Gallo Sauterne
    1 46 oz can grapefruit juice
    4 28 oz bottles ginger ale
    4 trays of ginger ale ice cubes or 2 boxes frozen
            strawberries
    1 lb fresh, canned or frozen peaches soaked 4 hours
            in brandy or 1 large can fruit cocktail

1. Put the brandy soaked peaches in a large punch bowl.
2. Add half the sauterne, chilled if possible.
3. Add half the grapefruit juice, chilled if possible.
4. Add 2 bottles ginger ale, chilled. Buy Vernors if you can get it—it has a very gingery taste.
5. Just before serving, add 2 trays ginger ale cubes or 1 box of frozen strawberries in a chunk.
6. When the punchbowl looks empty, add the remaining ingredients: 1/4 gallon of Sauterne, half the can of grapefruit juice, 2 bottles ginger ale, 2 trays of ginger ale ice cubes (or 1 box frozen strawberries).

I served a variation of this punch at my daughter's sweet sixteen party. I omitted the brandied peaches and substituted frozen fruit cocktail. I floated thin lemon slices in the punch which the kids ate. The wine is diluted enough to make the punch safe for sixteen year olds. At the same time, the wine is strong enough to make the punch festive. I felt better about giving them this punch than the usual soda pop.

Makes 2 punchbowls or serves 30—45

Wine Cooler

In the summer, we enjoy wine coolers. They are lighter and longer than wine and have a lovely, lemony taste.

jug of inexpensive wine of your choice
club soda
lemon wedges

1. To glass or pitcher of your choice add 1/2 red or white wine and 1/2 cold club soda. Squeeze juice from one or two lemon wedges.
2. Add ice cubes and lemon wedges.
3. Drink and enjoy.

Mint Julep

Moog makes a better mint julep than any I've ever tasted. This is a slooow sipping drink, not meant for sissies. The ice filled glass frosts and the mint smells grand. If you must sit and sweat, do it with a mint julep.

> 6 oz Bourbon
> 2 t powdered sugar
> Mint—4 sprigs
> Soda water

1. Fill glasses with crushed ice and set aside.
2. Put all mint leaves in a small deep bowl with sugar.
3. Mix with a wooden spoon to bruise leaves.
4. Add a bit of soda water, mix again, and add bourbon. Stir.
5. Strain into the prepared glasses over ice.
6. Work a long handled spoon up and down in the mixture until the glass begins to frost.
7. Taste and add more bourbon if desired.
8. Garnish with mint and serve.

Serves 2

Wines

We drink a lot of wine but only on rare occasions does a vintage bottle appear. Most of the time we drink good jug wine. Here are some of our favorites. We prefer dry wines.

JUG

Gallo Chablis Blanc
Gallo Hearty Burgundy
Italian Swiss Colony
Cabernet Sauvignon
Villa Banfi Roman White
Villa Banfi Roman Red
Sebastiani Barbera

MEDIUM PRICED WINES—DOMESTIC & IMPORTED

Bully Hill Red Wine—Dry
Bully Hill—Baco Noir—Dry Red
Bully Hill—Aurora Blanc—Dry White
Konstantine Franck—Joannesburg Riesling, 1971—Dry White
Cambas—Roditys—Dry Greek Rose
Cambas—Pendelli—Dry Greek Red
Ruffino or Brolio—Chianti
Bertani—Bardolino—Dry Red
Bertani—Valpolicella—White
Bertani—Soave—White

notes

notes

notes

notes

notes

notes

Index

A

Ancona, Italy, 158
antipasto, 29—30
apples, 154—187
   Apple—Ginger Jam, *142*
   Apple Raisin Nut Crepes, 22,24, *200*
   Apple Sausage Popovers, 21, *76*
   Fresh Apple Cake, 24, *168—69*
applesauce, 22, 91, *198*
apricot souffle, 27, 34, *182*
artichoke hearts, 31
   Artichoke Hearts Wrapped in Bacon, 37—39, *49*

B

Bach, 13
bagels, 42
Baklava, 25, *174—75*
Banana Kuchen, *154*
bananas, 187
bars, (*see* cookies)
basil, 5, 121
baskets, 12—13
Bay leaves, 5
bean sprouts, (*see* sprouts)
beef, 6, 80—82; roast, 43
  Oriental Beef & Carrots, 25, *81*
beer, 42, 79, 93
Bell Labs, 96
Billboard, 205
Biscuit Tortoni, 33, 37, 39, 192
blintzes, 21
  Mom's Blintzes, 22, *86—87*
bologna, 44
bowls, wooden, 12
Bran Muffins, 23, 35, 41, 134
Brasstown For Awhile, 160
Brasstown, N.C., 160
bread, (*see also* muffins, rolls, buns) *3*, 4, 9, 28,
  36, 38, 42, 44, 93; crumbs 8; chaleh 44;
  cocktail rye 37, 146; onion pockets 44;
  pumpernickel 3, 44; quick 3; rye 6, 37, 44,
  146; stale *8;* wheat 68; whole grain 79, 147;
  yeast 3, 21
Cheese Bread, 25, 28, 34, *138*
Cheese-Herb-Garlic Bread, *140*
Cornbread, 23, *131*

Garlic Bread, 23, 26, 28—29, 35, 39, 85, 98, *140*
  Herb Bread, 25—28, 33, 35, 75, 96, *139*
  Zucchini Bread, *141*
Bread Pudding, 8, 22, 184
breakfasts, *21—22,* 93
Briar Cove, N.C., 15—16
Broccoli with Cheese Sauce, 24, 83, *117*
broth, *8,* 67, 109
buckwheat groats, (*see* kasha)
budget, 19, 40, 46
Buffalo, N.Y., 39, 51
buffets, 14, 20, *27—28, 33—35, 43—48,* 49, 93
buns,
  Sticky Buns, *136*
butter, *4,* 28, 36, 45, 86, 91, 93, 96; curry 118;
  lemon 118; orange 118

C

cabbage,
  Cole Slaw, *125*
  Stuffed Cabbage Rolls, 6, 23, *78—79*
cabinets, 13, *15—16*
Cage, John, 56—57
cake (*see also* cheesecake), *151, 154, 156—73,*
  176; coffee 42; pound 26, 162, 172; sheet
  40; spice 168, 173; stale 8
  Banana Kuchen, *154*
  Custard & Marmalade Filled Rum Cake, 26,
  158
  Fresh Apple Cake, 24, 168—69
  Fudge Pie, *155*
  Great Grandma's Spongecake, *176*
  Italian Rum Cake, *157—59*
  Marble Turban Cake, *162*
  Mini Chip Cake, *166*
  Poor Man's Cake, 22, 173
  Royal Pound Cake, *172*
  Sister Mildred's Cream Cheese Coffee Cake, 28,
  171
    Sour Cream Chocolate Cake, *167*
    Strawberry Nut Torte, *164—65*
    Tosca Cake, 24, 160—61
    Walnut Torte, 32, *156*
    Zabaglione Filled Rum Cake, 35, *158*
candy (*see also* fudge), toronne, 29